Directions

How to Live a Full Life and Leave a Legacy

James Attrell

Clovercroft Publishing

Directions: How to Live a Full Life and Leave a Legacy

© 2018 by James Attrell

Published by Clovercroft Publishing, Franklin, Tennessee

Scripture quotation from the New Revised Standard Version Bible, copyright © 1989 the Division of Christian Education of the National Council of the Churches of Christ in the United States of America. Used by permission. All rights reserved.

Senior Editor: Tammy Kling

Associate Editor: Tiarra Tompkins

Copy Editor: Lee Titus Elliott

Cover Designer: Suzanne Elliott

Illustration and Interior Layout Designer: Adept Content Solutions

Printed in the United States of America

ISBN: 978-1-948484-03-9

You cannot legislate the poor into freedom by legislating the wealthy out of freedom. What one person receives without working for, another person must work for without receiving. The government cannot give to anybody anything that the government does not first take from somebody else. When half of the people get the idea that they do not have to work because the other half is going to take care of them, and when the other half gets the idea that it does no good to work because somebody else is going to get what they work for, that my dear friend, is about the end of any nation. You cannot multiply wealth by dividing it.

— Adrian Rogers, https://youtu.be/xgJKR0o4RhU

Contents

Introduction

Have you ever thought about which attributes should lead our lives, and which should follow? Are you logical and protective, or creative and compassionate? Should feelings take priority, or thoughts and ideas?

These are questions I explored for many years, navigating through my travels and experiences.

As an immigrant from Canada who's traveled the world, including every single continent (yes, even to Antarctica), I can tell you with certainty that I live in the best country in the world and the best state (Texas) bar none. And that includes Canada (specifically the province of Alberta), my home country that will always remain close to my heart. It took a dozen years through the legal process to proudly become an American citizen on Feb 6, 1992, in the courthouse at Sherman, Texas.

In addition to my traveling, I have also experienced pretty much every major life event that you can imagine. Just name one, and I have likely participated in it. I've lived through marriage, births, divorce, cancer, arthritis, and car wrecks. Job loss, foreclosure, bankruptcy, adoption, and the death of loved ones, including a parent and young sibling, have all touched my life. I've experienced tornadoes, hurricanes, tropical storms, and earthquakes. Extraordinary experiences live in my memories, from political elections, significant weight loss, quitting smoking, building a lake, flying small planes and drones, and traveling to famous world-wide attractions. I've served on nonprofit boards, served as a bank director, served as a city councilman, served as a Boy Scout leader, served as a hockey coach, helped to organize silent auctions, and went without a cell phone for an entire weekend. Yup, been there; done that.

I also learned how to capture my journey photographically and on paper.

Over my years as an amateur photo and video buff, I managed to collect quite an extensive library of family video on all mediums that existed from the 1960s to date. That included my father's super eight video and the very first VHS tapes. I decided to convert all that video over to digital format and to create an iTunes library of every second of that video. The process was somewhat complicated. First, I copied the video to DVDs. I set each medium to copy to DVDs, one at a time and one each night. That took about a year, but the process occurred while I slept. All I had to do was remember to change out the video medium and install a new DVD and to label the just-completed DVD.

Next, I installed each DVD, one each night, into my Mac computer and saved the video as an MPEG file onto my newly acquired and very large (24 TB) hard drive. That took another year, but, once again, it all happened while I slept. Finally, I transferred each new movie file into iTunes and created libraries by date so that I could use iMovie to create edited movies for any family event, such as video memories of one of my children for a high school graduation, or a birthday.

Life is a collection of stories, and people, knitted together. You travel somewhere, meet interesting people, tell them a story, and they carry that story with them for a lifetime. Chances are they pass it on, which in turn passes on a piece of your life to someone unknown, in another town or country. Each one of us positively impacts the world if we want to. If you truly want to make a difference on this planet, it's not that hard.

The family movie process took just a few weeks. Now, I can scroll through over fifty years of family video history in moments, and the memories have become a reminder that I really need to write this book, because future generations will likely not want to watch some 300 hours of "home movies." If you do, just let me know.

I feel that, somewhere in all those endless hours of entertainment, there are anchors that will help others during stormy times. If this book helps others hook onto those anchors, or helps them get to where they are going, then I will have done my job and fulfilled my journey.

With the experiences contained in this book, I hope that I can inspire and motivate you. I hope to inspire my family, friends, and even unknown friends and future generations to positively impact the world that we live in.

Life

One evening, an elderly Cherokee brave told his grandson about a battle that goes on inside people. "My son, the Battle is between two wolves inside us all. One is Evil manifesting itself as anger, regret, and fear. The other is Good. It brings about joy, peace, and hope," he said. The grandson thought about it for a moment and then asked his grandfather, "Which one wins?" The old Cherokee simply replied, "The one that you feed."

And if you remember nothing else then remember these wise words from an ancient proverb:

He who knows not, and knows not that he knows not, is a fool; shun him.

He who knows not, and knows that he knows not, is a child; teach him.

He who knows, and knows not that he knows, is asleep; wake him.

He who knows, and knows that he knows, is wise; follow him.

"Life is like riding a bicycle. To stay in balance, you must keep moving."

—Albert Einstein

Chapter 1

Water, Haiti, and Prosperity

From Haiti to Singapore and from Alaska to the Antarctic, clean water plays a most crucial role in the health of human life everywhere that it exists. Where there is clean drinking water, you generally find peace and prosperity. Where water is scarce, you will often find strife and conflict.

Over 90 percent of the fresh water in the world is found in the ice fields of the Antarctic and Greenland, with the Antarctic fresh water dwarfing that of the Greenland ice sheets.

Eight hundred million people live without access to clean drinking water.

Unsafe water and lack of basic sanitation cause more deaths each year than all forms of violence, including war. Children are especially vulnerable, given their small bodies, which can't handle the intense dehydration from diarrheal disease. In developing countries, women and children collect water for their families. They often walk miles each day to the nearest source, which is often unprotected and whose water is therefore likely to make them sick. Time spent at this chore keeps children from attending school, working, or taking care of their families.

Haiti is surrounded by salt water and has ample fresh groundwater just a few feet below the surface. Two years after the 7.0 magnitude earthquake struck Haiti in 2010, I served on a mission in Grand-Goave and saw firsthand how new water wells change the lives of many who suffered through cholera and other serious diseases.

Singapore, one of my favorite places to visit, is also surrounded by salt water, but it is one of the most modern and advanced nations in the world. It is in the process of transitioning from piped water from

Malaysia to other more modern and reliable water sources, such as rainwater harvesting, desalination of seawater, and conversion of grey-water sewage to drinking water.

Before that last thought makes you sick, that system is very successful in many places, including Wichita Falls, Texas (https://youtu.be/gTsYuOcJIts). What is the difference between Haiti and Singapore? Why is there such a difference in the quality of life? Is it the lack of leadership in the past, or is it because of contentment with and acceptance of poor conditions?

Imagine visiting a country that has no street addresses and where possession of property is considered ownership. These situations in Haiti are remnants from past slavery of the Haitians by the French, who stripped the country of its beautiful forests, as well as its very dignity, and who introduced voodoo and all its evil (https://youtu.be/cKW53FrLMq8).

Next door to Haiti, on the very same Caribbean island, is the Dominican Republic. Why does it have the ninth largest economy in Latin America and an upper-middle income from agriculture, mining, and tourism, while Haiti remains far behind economically and socially and in much distress?

Could it be that the Spanish, who controlled the Dominican Republic, encouraged trade and free markets and thus liberated the people, who then built businesses that prospered and created employment and wealth?

When it comes down to survival, do you draw from faith, or do you draw from fear? Free people become ingenious if left to their own devices (absent oppressive government intervention) because worry disrupts productivity and hope never disappoints. John Paul Jones is quoted as saying, "If fear is cultivated, it will become stronger; if faith is cultivated, it will achieve mastery."

A people reliant on their government for anything beyond a safe and secure country, with efficient transportation systems, will start to lose the ability to think for themselves, and they will not seek prosperity.

In Haiti, self-government has not yet taken hold; the people do not feel safe and secure, and efficient transportation systems are close to nonexistent. It might be several generations before Christianity replaces voodoo, but that process is underway. I have seen firsthand the positive results in some of the communities in Haiti and the much-needed, but struggling, business environment.

Haiti Arise is building orphanages, and its medical facility and schools serve a community that strives to be joyful while learning how to deal with sorrow rather than living in sorrow and instead seeking joy (https://youtu.be/YZ5HwqOQjoI).

Marc and Lisa Honorat are encouraging Haitians to make different lifestyle choices, which are leading to positive results. That's hard to beat when word gets around. During my visit, we traveled into town for supplies, and a rear wheel of our mission van fell through the road surface into an open sewage enclosure. Before I could gather up my photographic equipment and exit the van along with the others, a stranger jumped into the driver's seat and started rocking the van back and forth. I looked out the rear window, and about ten-to-fifteen strangers were pushing on the van and rocking it out of the hole in the street surface.

Within minutes, the van was back on the road, and the strangers disappeared as rapidly as they had appeared. You see, in spite of voodoo influences, the people in the community were fearful of God and saw firsthand the positive forces of Haiti Arise. The van proudly displayed the mission sign, and at once I understood just what Pastor Marc meant when he said, "You will be safe here as long as you are with me and people know that you are part of the efforts of the Haiti Arise mission."

The message was clear. Do no harm. Do only good. Love and help others. It's not complicated. Marc and Lisa believe that, in order to catch a lot, you need to catch a few, repeatedly. That is a lesson that works in all aspects of life. Set a target. Do a little every day, and you will arrive at your destination eventually.

Chapter 2

China

About half of the world's population get fresh water from the Tibetan plateau and its many glaciers. Yes, that is half of the world's population. Is it any wonder that China wants to maintain control of Tibet?

The Chinese say it will take about twenty plus years before they can start to reduce harmful emissions into the atmosphere. The flip side is that the emissions will continue to increase for twenty years. With a fast-growing population and the recent acceptance of two-children families, new electrical-energy sources are needed in order to replace coal-burning power plants, which are the primary polluters.

The Chinese have piped in natural gas from Russia and are converting some of the coal-burning power plants to this much cleaner source of energy. Also, they are building hydroelectric dams in Tibet to provide for the growing population in China. However, while the dams are under construction, water flow to India and other countries is restricted, thus creating drought conditions in those areas.

One of my more fascinating journeys was a week that I spent with a large group of photographers on a trip across China and Tibet to Nepal lead by very experienced National Geographic tour guides. We arrived in Kathmandu a few months before the earthquake destroyed the city, and I am very grateful that I was able to photograph many special temples and memorials prior to their destruction.

We visited a village in Tibet and spent several hours in a home consisting of grandparents, a wife, husbands, and children. Yes, I said, husbands. In these older villages on the Tibetan plateau, the mother is in charge of the household. It's an ancient custom that the family selects a woman to marry their sons (and that can range from one up to three or four sons) and that she moves into the family's home and takes charge.

Tiananmen Square

Tibet

Children born in this family are not certain who exactly is their father, but they grow up having specific chores and duties. There are no trees at this altitude, so they heat their home and cook their meals using dung from their yak herd. That herd lives on the first floor of the home during cold spells and at night. Gathering dung and preparing it for use is an important task.

The mother is in charge of the solar cooker, which she keeps in the middle open area of the second floor, where the bedrooms are, as well as the other living areas. That cooker uses solar heating and sits within a metal stand containing reflective panels as a heat source. She carefully moves the metal stand as the sun rotates across the sky, heating the stew contained therein.

Water is piped into a common area by gravity in surface-mounted plastic piping. This area is also used to hand wash clothes in a daily community woman's club meeting. From what I saw, the water flow would likely freeze in the pipe at night in the winter, but it would be quickly thawed out by the sun during the day. That pipe ran a very long distance to a lake in the hills, and I was pretty certain that it was carefully monitored and maintained by the village leaders.

The base camp on the north face of Mount Everest was a windy and frigid place. It took several hours to drive there in four-wheel-drive jeeps. There were no real roads on the trip, but the guides made this journey on a regular basis and knew where to go and how to handle the many challenges that we faced as we traveled. New rivers would appear where previously there were none, and, for the most part, we felt as if we were traveling on the moon around giant rocks and over terrain absent any vegetation.

The guides said that there would not likely be any cell phone communication, but when we reached the base camp at 16,931 feet, I was able to crawl under a

Mount Everest Base Camp

large rock to get out of the wind and call my daughter, Marissa, and my granddaughter, Delilah, on iPhone Facetime and to show them the landscape. It was an exciting and special memory that will be difficult to equal in my lifetime.

Some say that I try to do too much and that I should slow down and smell the roses. That would be my wife and the love of my life, Sherry Lynne Stewart.

It is true that I set my goals high and that I try to squeeze every ounce of the juice out of my life. I believe that aiming for a higher level of achievement in life is healthy because gravity, as the saying goes, will likely impact your result when you least expect it. Had I not disregarded the guide who said that cell phone usage was not likely at the base camp, I might not have tried!

The good things we do, the significant things, are always challenging. Life is too full of opportunities to suffer and be miserable, so why not be hopeful in all that we do? The future shouldn't just stand there, waving you in! The Bible tells us to be strong and courageous. We should be the best version of ourselves in all that we do.

Pulling out my cell phone from my warm pocket required removal of my warm gloves in a fierce and cold windstorm and then the partial removal of my winter parka. Then I had to manipulate the small buttons on the phone with now-frozen fingers and dial the correct numbers to Texas from Mount Everest—all while the guide was telling me that I was wasting my time. You get the drift. It would have been much easier (and warmer) to listen to the experts and blindly follow their lead.

Now, having written that, I realize that I just condemned the very people who brought me safely up the dangerous and treacherous slopes of a majestic mountain in the middle of nowhere. Nothing can be further from the truth. What I did was to listen very carefully to how they answered my question about cell phone usage at the base camp.

What the lead guide said is that he had once experienced some cell phone usage at the base camp but that I should not expect it. What was the risk of giving it a try? Cold hands? That's all? Of course, an answered prayer for help, and that is my message. Hope matters, and so does prayer, but action doesn't hurt, either.

Traveling through Tibet was fascinating, as we learned all about the political and religious history of the region. Because our tour bus contained more than a dozen travelers, we were required to stop and pick up an armed Chinese police officer, who traveled on our bus with us. The bus itself had an alarm that alerted the driver and us when he was speeding. Our guide explained that video cameras covered all traffic and walkways and that, with an advanced facial recognition system, the Chinese police did not need to be patrolling any area of the country.

Criminals are therefore easily located and arrested, and even second-offender speeders would disappear and spend time in lengthy "training" sessions while imprisoned. Families would often be unaware of the location of missing relatives. They would (hopefully) just show up one day.

After making the eventful and adventurous journey through Tibet and stopping at the numerous Chinese inspection stations along the way, where we had to produce our itinerary and passports over and over again, we descended rapidly to Kathmandu. There had been an earthquake in the area several months before our arrival, causing the road to be destroyed. The temporary road lacked protective barriers and, for the most part, was only wide enough for one-way travel. At one point, the road was shut down where a truck hung dangerously over the edge, awaiting rescue by a tow truck.

When we arrived at the Nepal border, there was a very long line of cargo trucks, waiting for Chinese inspection at the border crossing. The entire contents of each truck were removed and inspected and then placed by hand in a cargo truck on the Nepal side of the border. Nothing left Tibet (China) until it was thoroughly inspected, and that included our group.

On our last day there, we hired a small aircraft specializing in flights around Mount Everest. It was an incredible flight. Many beautiful mountains surround Mount Everest. Mount Everest just happens to be the tallest (https://youtu.be/xaf9Wgx-J1E).

Chapter 3

My Grandparents

As a child, my fondest memories were the times we visited my paternal grandparents' small home on a farm in Carstairs, Alberta, where they lived much of their senior years. We would gather there regularly, along with uncles and aunts and many cousins, as well as other friends and more distant family members at times. Somehow, that little house on the prairie did not seem small to me, although I am sure that our parents found it to be rather crowded.

My grandmother, Helen Attrell, was a strong woman, both emotionally and physically, and she was able to manage my wheelchair-bound grandfather, Steve Attrell, without any help quite late into senior life. She would equip us with a .22 caliber rifle and teach us how to shoot the gophers destroying her very large farm garden.

Grandma Helen always remembered to make potatoes and gravy for me, even if she served something different for everyone else. When she caught me smoking in the farm garage, along with my cousin John and Uncle Bob, she threatened to take us to family court if she found us smoking again. We had no idea what that meant, but we made sure to smoke elsewhere after that. She always mowed the grassy field before our arrival so that we could have our family football game, where everyone participated.

Grandpa Steve was a First World War amputee and a hero. He served with the Canadian Corps at the brutal battles of Passchendaele and Vimy Ridge in France and then survived the Spanish Flu. These fierce, ground, hand-to-hand battles took place just across the English Channel, where he was born, south of London, England, in Godstone, Surrey, in 1896.

He loved crib and card games, and although he had severe arthritis in his hands, he would never pass on shuffling or dealing. He also loved to paint and spent his later years working tirelessly through his difficulties in managing a paintbrush to complete several beautiful, paint-by-number works of art. What I learned from him is that things are never as bad as they seem and that endurance builds and supports character. Beethoven's best works emerged from his senior years, when he was deaf. Imagine that!

My great-grandfather Dick (my dad's grandfather) outlived three wives. I have only a faint memory of him. He lived to age nighty-eight. What I remember most is his passing out peppermints to the kids and turning off his hearing aid when we arrived.

I never felt poor or lacking of anything, but I do remember that I had just two pairs of pants. One pair of dress pants and one for everyday use. Mom would wash my pants on Sunday, when I wore my dress pants to church. I also remember that my family could only afford powdered milk at times. It tasted chalky, and unlike anything we'd ever tasted before. It certainly didn't resemble milk. I also remember that we would go for days alternating between spaghetti and cheese and spaghetti and tomatoes at the dinner table. Pasta was a staple that got us through the lean times.

Chapter 4

Paperboy Lessons

I was encouraged to work at an early age, and, at age eleven, I had a paper route earning enough money to support my camera and photo hobby and to grow my coin collection. I learned that equality of opportunity meant that I could replace relaxation and fun with hard work and could earn money for what I wanted out of life. My lazy friends relied on what their parents could afford to dole out, while I managed to have money for my hobby, but I always made sure that there was some left over for the future. In 1968, at age seventeen, I was able to buy my first car.

The harder you work, the more you earn, and the more likely it is that you can be a blessing to others. You don't have to have money to be a blessing to others. Money is just a different kind of blessing that you silently and secretly use to help others, as the Bible directs us to do.

I have many good memories of my life as a *Calgary Herald* newspaper boy. Technically, I was supposed to be twelve years old when I applied for my paper route, but I believe that no one else applied for the position, so I gave it a shot at age eleven (almost twelve).

In the extreme southern limits of Calgary was Southwood, and my first route included fewer than thirty homes to begin with, because Southwood was a new residential neighborhood. The neighborhood grew quickly to over 100 homes, and, over the three-to-four years that I had the route, it was divided up several times, but I always had my choice of delivery zone. On Saturday mornings, I would walk or ride the bus, depending on the weather, to the downtown *Calgary Herald* office to pay my bill, a distance of about 100 blocks, followed by a visit to the pool halls to advance my skills. My best memories were those of Monday small-page quantity papers, where I could fit them all in one bag on the handlebars of my bicycle.

Grandpa Upton and Jennifer

Grandma Attrell Siblings

Grandpa and Grandma Upton,
Doreen, Audrey and Roy

Grandma Attrell Five generations

Grandpa Attrell with Ken Attrell sons

Grandpa and Grandma Attrell, Ken

16

Grandpa Attrell

cousins John, Cathy and Jim at family grave plot of Great Grandfather Joseph Attrell and Great Grandmother Blanche Attrell near Red Deer, Alberta

Grandpa and Grandma Attrell with Children Doug, Bob, Connie and Ken

Grandpa Upton and Grandpa Attrell

Standing - Grandma Helen, Mother Doreen, Father Doug, Grandpa Steve, Sitting - Jim, Great Grandpa Dick, Brother Kim and seated - Uncle Bob

My worst memories were those of Saturday large-page quantity papers that needed delivery in temperatures of forty degrees below zero and three or four feet of snow. I would get so miserable that I would deliver a number of papers and then return home to thaw out before continuing to deliver them in the biting cold. I nearly froze my fingers, toes, and ears so often that they are very sensitive to freezing temperatures to this day. That might be all in my head, but that's where it counts. Right?!

My brother, Kim, took over my route until his death in a car-and-train wreck in 1968, at which time Peter, my youngest brother, took over the route. My sister, Patsy, would occasionally help, as would some of her friends. In good weather, I could always find someone younger, which I could enslave for a short time. One of my earliest investing experiences was purchasing Canada Savings Bonds with my savings, putting them in a safe deposit box, and clipping the dividend coupons when they became due.

The concept of "mailbox" money and recurring revenue really hit home at an early age. I also learned that in order to catch a lot, you will need to catch a little, repeatedly. Rome wasn't built overnight, and neither was any worthwhile endeavor. I learned to set a goal and to do a little to advance towards my goal every day. Of course, having a written goal or one that you can express in definitive but straightforward terms is important. The goal, "I want to be a doctor," or, "I want to travel," or "I want children," is not definitive. The goal, "I want to be a pediatrician," or, "I want to visit London and Beijing," or, "I want to marry and have two kids," is getting closer to a clear definition.

Think it out, and think it daily. Push that massive boulder towards the cliff just a little every day. You'll get there one day. I wrote this book on the note application of my iPhone. A chapter at a time. Just remember that if you don't have goals that match your God-given reason for existence, then you will be running for a finish line that doesn't exist.

Chapter 5

Responsibility

As I traveled around the world, I learned that almost all the capital that was used to create and build churches, parks, schools, museums, and monuments came from the charitable donations of hard-working people who started successful businesses and created wealth for themselves and others, while creating jobs for many. These individuals discovered their God-given talents, and they inspired others to join their organizations, creating even more jobs. More important, they supported worthwhile causes to realize God's promise of prosperity to those who share and bless others by their actions.

These individuals often had to battle with the politics of envy and income inequality. While they strove to lift people up to higher ground, liberal politicians worked to knock them down and steal their hard-earned income through excessive taxation, not understanding that people of means create jobs and prosperity for all. These business owners also offer the opportunity to all to realize the American Dream. Their children are usually raised to understand that equal opportunity is important but that any attempt to get equal results will fail, because that attempt will create and nurture a culture of dependence and entitlement. Victimhood, mediocrity, and anger result, instead of ability and hope. We mustn't deny the successful crowd of the positive consequences of their choices. As ye sow, so shall ye reap.

You won't meet these wealthy, behind-the-scenes people on Wall Street. Wall Street represents relatively few businesses in America and represents only the largest of corporations that are publicly traded. Wall Street is the place where pension funds invest the savings of retired citizens, who worked hard all of their lives and who rely on the growth and dividends offered by such investments. Wall Street is for big business and for big banks, and it is not a place for the inexperienced.

I speak from experience and from several years of intensive training in economics and the worldwide futures, forex, options, and equities markets. I also have extensive training from personal experience in the U.S. real estate market.

Wall Street is a large casino where only the largest institutions can thrive, given the impact of computer programs and automated methods of transferring wealth from retail customers (the sheep) to the big banks (the wolves) and other such investor institutions that prey on the unsuspecting. The day of buying and holding the stock of quality corporations seems to have become a thing of the past. Manipulation of the price of currencies, commodities, and equities by big banks and government seems to have become the new normal. So enter the casino at your own risk.

That being said, I'm suggesting that you should save your money and invest wisely.

You absolutely should do so. Just make certain that you are investing and not gambling. There is a thin line between the two. There is another bitcoin or marijuana stock investment waiting just around the corner at all times. Like the 1800s gold rush or multilevel marketing schemes, the money flows from the pockets of the foolish to the bank accounts of the corrupt.

The vast majority of Americans do not work for Wall Street corporations. On the contrary, most Americans work for privately held companies. These smaller corporations make a lot of their own rules, and they are the real backbone of our country.

Most of our politicians are lawyers who do not understand basic economics. If a business does not earn a profit for the owners, then it must cut costs, and that usually means job loss. On the other hand, these same businesses will utilize excess earnings to grow and create jobs. That action, however, is entirely the owners' prerogative, as it should be.

After all, they put their capital at risk to create and grow their business; therefore, it is their right to manage excess cash flow in whatever way that they wish. In many cases, that excess cash flow becomes a "rainy day" fund to protect the business and sustain the employment of people in the event of a catastrophe. If only all governments acted in that way (the State of Texas does), along with businesses, and built a "rainy day" fund. Such a fund ensures that you live within your means.

John Wesley said it best when he instructed us to earn, save, and give all that you can.

One of my favorite stories that hits home to my message is about an ant. The ant worked hard in the withering heat and the rain all summer long, building his house and laying up supplies for the winter.

The grasshopper thought that the ant was a fool and laughed and danced and played the summer away. Come winter, the shivering grasshopper called a press conference and demanded to know why the ant should be allowed to be warm and well fed, while he was cold and starving. All the liberal media showed up to provide pictures of the shivering grasshopper next to a video of the ant in his comfortable home, with a table filled with food.

American viewers were stunned by the sharp contrast. How can this be, that in a country of such wealth, this poor grasshopper is allowed to suffer so? Kermit the Frog appeared on CNN, along with the grasshopper, and all the American viewers cried when they sang, "It's Not Easy Being Green." People Against Poverty staged a demonstration in front of the ant's house, while the left-wing news stations filmed the group singing, "We Shall Overcome." Then President Obama declared a national day of mourning to be celebrated annually for the grasshopper's sake and so that Americans would have a day off to contemplate the plight of the grasshopper. Harry Reid condemned the ant and blamed the Republicans. Senator Bernie Sanders and Secretary of State Hillary Clinton explained in an interview that the ant got rich off the back of the grasshopper, and both called for an immediate tax hike on the ant to make him pay his fair share.

Finally, the Democrats drafted the Economic Equity and Anti-Grasshopper Act retroactive to the beginning of the summer. The ant was fined for failing to hire a proportionate number of green bugs and having nothing left to pay his retroactive taxes; his home was confiscated by the federal government's green czar and given to the grasshopper.

The story ends as we see the grasshopper and his free-loading friends finishing up the last bits of the ant's food, while the government house he was in, which, as you recall, just happens to be the ant's old house, crumbled around them, because the grasshopper didn't maintain it.

The ant disappeared in the snow, never to be seen again. The grasshopper was found dead in a drug-related incident, and the house, now abandoned, was taken over by a gang of spiders, who terrorized and plundered the once-prosperous and once-peaceful neighborhood. The end! (https://youtu.be/ripQ9jJnw1c).

This story sounds like Detroit in the beginning of its collapse as a city, doesn't it? And for those who don't know, this is pretty much the story of the once-prosperous City of Detroit.

Just remember that government's first priority is supposed to be to protect its citizens. Democracy is not giving away free stuff for politicians to get elected.

Chapter 6

America

Josh and Marissa with Delilah and Eloise

You could travel the world, as I did, and chances are you'd still miss America, as I did.

America is the freest and most dynamic society in history.

Freedom and equality of outcome have never coexisted anywhere else at anytime. The innovator, the first mover, the talented, and the most persistent win out, producing large income inequality. The prizes are unequal, because in, America's system, consumers reward people for the value that they add. Some can and do add extraordinary value, others can't or don't or simply choose not to, and that is okay. Income is 24 percent less equally distributed in America compared to the income of most of the modern industrialized countries. But America has a 42 percent higher income per capita and household wealth 210 percent higher than those same countries.

Do you suppose that Americans would give up 42 percent of their own income in an effort to take from the wealthy? That has been the direction of the Democrats who have controlled the White House and Congress for most of the last ten years prior to President Trump's inauguration on January 20, 2017, and that explains why, as a percentage, there are fewer Americans working today than there were ten years ago.

I have traveled the world, often alone.

Many people have asked why Sherry did not accompany me on my many world travels. And I respond that while she has physical issues that make travel painful and unpleasant, I really do not mind traveling alone. And, on several occasions, I have invited my brother Peter and my sister Patsy to join me.

As a male traveling alone, I can find that chocolate is just another snack, and I can wear a white T-shirt whenever I want; I'm always in the same mood (except when I'm hungry or tired), and conversations are thirty seconds flat. Not only is life simple when you're traveling alone; traveling by yourself is also a journey into your soul. Too many people get married and never spend time understanding themselves and who they are. They don't have time to think, pray, or truly know what their God-given purpose is, because their days and nights are covered in the clutter of activity. Traveling alone is a wonderful way to discover yourself again.

I travel with everything in a carry-on bag: one pair of shoes works fine, I can wear shorts anytime; I can trim my nails with a pocket knife; the color of clothing is not important; I don't need to shave; shopping takes five minutes or fewer. I need just six items or fewer in the bathroom when I travel. Contrast that with Sherry; she brings along stuff that I can't identify, let alone pronounce.

Chapter 7

Argentina

On my way to the Antarctic, I spent a couple of days in Buenos Aries, Argentina, for some guided sight-seeing and a river cruise. My guide told me the story about the severe impact that the depression and currency devaluation of the early 1990s had on her family. Her father had saved for his retirement and the education of his children, but he held his savings in cash that was now suddenly devalued by an Argentinian government whose debt was unsustainable. The country was insolvent and defaulted on its debt, which meant that her father ended up with next to nothing and could no longer support his family, along with millions of others.

Her father's best friend went through the same process, but, rather than cash investments, he held real estate that became extremely valuable as a result of the government's devaluing the currency and therefore making his net worth very large. This friend ended up supporting the family and other families through those terrible times. Life is full of such storms and chaos, but, ultimately, it will be all right, as evidenced by this instance of panic turning to peace.

Chapter 8

Boy Scouts

Boy Scouts learn about the importance of preparation, and although I learned how to tie knots, build campfires, grab snakes by the tail (so I wouldn't get bitten) and live outside in a winter storm, the most important thing I learned was to prepare for the unexpected. A plane stays in the sky only as long as it has a pilot and fuel, and so it is with life. It is true that the early bird gets the worm. Just make sure you are the early bird, and not the early worm.

Our family attended Kingsland Baptist Church in Calgary, Canada, where I became a Boy Scout, and that church is also where I married my high school sweetheart, Judy Sundell, at age 18, after learning that she was pregnant with my daughter Jennifer. Jennifer's birth was one of the very special memories of my youth. She brought joy and meaning to my life. At least until she became a teenager.

My brother Kim died in a car-and-train collision in 1968, and my parents had a drinking fountain installed in the basement of he church in his memory, along with a plaque. Years later, the church underwent a major renovation, and the drinking fountain, along with the plaque, was dumped in the trash. One of the construction superintendents rescued the plaque and gave it to a news reporter. That news reporter did some research on the plaque and the name "Attrell" and called me to see if I knew Kim. Now, as I get older, I have come to see coincidence as a miracle. When this person from the newspaper called, Mom happened to be in Calgary, visiting from Nanaimo, British Columbia, and she consented to an interview and received the plaque. It made for a great family-interest story in the *Calgary Herald*.

After being a Cub Scout and a Boy Scout at the church, I was asked to return as temporary Scout master until the group committee found a permanent Scout master. After a couple of years of mostly outdoor camping and related scouting leadership, I asked to be relieved of the task, because my sons, Chris and Tim, entered the Scout scene and I needed to work part-time to support my family. In fact, I had to work full-time at Atco Leasing, as well as part-time at Corbett's Wholesale and at various gas stations to pay the bills.

Chapter 9

Pumping Gas

Being a gas jockey taught me many important life lessons. After I gave up my paper route to my brother at age sixteen, I started working at Southwood Texaco and then Southwood Royalite in Calgary, after being fired from Southwood for driving the tow truck drunk on a Sunday afternoon service trip and after the customer reported me to the owner. My only excuse at the time was that my brother had just died and that I felt bad. Although I did feel bad, I was doing as many seventeen-year-old kids will do: experimenting with a new (illegal) liquor-delivery system that operated on Sundays (also illegal). That my (much older) workmate at the gas station was a bit of an alcoholic probably didn't help matters. He later committed suicide by starting up his car in his garage and leaving the overhead door shut. He left six young children behind. That was my first experience with untreated depression. He never talked about it much, but when he did, it quickly became apparent that he was bitter about his lot in life.

George, the owner at the Texaco station, called me back the next day after having fired me, apologized for not understanding my grief reaction, and asked me to come back to work. However, by that time, I had settled into a new job with new friends and was working within two blocks of home.

My sister Tricia used to bring me lunch occasionally, and I remember her asking me what I really liked. Not knowing why she asked, I said, "Blue cheese," which resulted in six slices of bread covered in blue cheese for lunch, which she delivered and watched me (painfully) eat.

Chapter 10

Running Away from Home

I snuck out the basement window of our home one evening, determined that I would run away to Edmonton (200 miles north) by Greyhound Bus and start life anew as a fifteen-year-old in a strange city that was also the city of my birth. The argument with my parents was over something minor, because I have no memory of the reason for my youthful decision. I do remember dreaming constantly about setting out on my own when school was completed. Patsy heard me leaving and chased me, asking where I was going. I told her that I was leaving for awhile but that I would be back one day. After a policeman found me on a park bench in Edmonton that night, I was escorted back to the bus station, and he stood there with me until I boarded the bus and took the four-hour trip back to Calgary. I was home sooner than expected, and, with all the hustle and bustle in a home with four kids (I was the oldest), no one but my sister noticed that I had returned because no one had noticed that I was gone.

I think that the spirit of adventure has always run in my veins and that I may have left home simply because I could. I wonder how may life decisions I made in that manner during my more youthful years.

Chapter 11

Australia

If there is a place that I might return for another visit, it would be Sidney Harbour in Australia. Without any type of visible heavy industry, it features a much-used boat-taxi system with numerous stops at housing, restaurants, shopping, parks, and commercial office buildings, where many of the residents work. The weather is so pleasant year-round that restaurants are open-air, with shutters that the close up at night when the restaurants close.

My visit to the Blue Mountains was a guided tour, and I was able to experience trailing kangaroos and other unique wildlife through the forests. Phillip Island featured a grandstand that held over 100 tourists at sundown, when the twelve- to eighteen-inch penguins returned to the seashore from a day of fishing. They had to wait until sundown to walk up the beach to their burrows and caves in the hills, because the seagulls would peck their heads and cause them to throw up the meal that they were bringing home to their penguin family. We watched in silence as they waddled past us in the dark, like short little soldiers on a mission. Occasionally, one would linger behind, so the group would circle back and wait for their friend. These penguin parents would take turns, on alternating days, to make the long journey and daily fishing trip. What a life lesson for new parents and sharing the workload! Equal "yoking" by parents is necessary—and not just in the animal world but by humans, as well.

It was interesting to know that the Australian government has abolished its carbon tax because of the tax's negative impact on its economy. Australia is larger than the United States in land mass, but a very small portion of it is populated. It has about the same population as Canada, and, like Canada, it is very reliant on commodity production and sales to China, the country that dwarfs Australia in both population and pollution (https://youtu.be/GMxOPT78Sy8).

Chapter 12

The Equator

Crossing the equator by cruise ship had been a bucket-list adventure, and I turned it into a personal experience forever etched in my memory. As we were sailing around Indonesia, the cruise director announced that we were soon crossing the equator and that we would celebrate by staging a dance and celebration on the upper deck

Jim at the Equator

at the time of crossing, which director announced as 2:00 p.m.

Fortunately, I had downloaded and practiced with an iPhone app called "My Altitude," which provided instant information that included my exact GPS location. In checking the application, it was evident that we would be crossing the equator much earlier than indicated by the cruise director, so I set the app to take multiple selfie photos as we actually crossed the equator, complete with GPS location overlay inscribed on each photo. I was fortunate to photograph the exact moment of crossing with the ship pool deck in the background. The exact GPS coordinates were 0-0-0 N and 119-2-39 E as recorded on the photograph.

Running down to my room afterward, I checked the direction of the drain water in my sink, and, contrary to what I was told, the water still swirled clockwise down the drain. So much for that assumption. Perhaps I needed to wait awhile.

Another highlight of the trip was visiting Bali and participating in an elephant safari. If you have never ridden on an elephant, I highly recommend the experience. We also visited the only places (Indonesian islands) where the Komodo dragon exists. These large reptiles can chase down a grown man, and our guides approached them with large, forked sticks to hold them back if the raced toward us. They hunt and live off a diet of deer and other smaller animals that once they are bitten by the dragon, they die from the poisonous bite.

Jim white river rafting in Indonesia

I exercised extreme caution with my video and photography, in spite of the guides' assurances. I kept thinking, "Trust but verify," something I learned (the hard way) when building our business. With an underlying fear of death, I tend to avoid the unknown when it comes to my safety, and you won't catch me parachuting out of an airplane unless I am lucky enough to reach an advanced age.

One of my more educated guides was a Hindu and said that President Obama was very popular in Indonesia and that he was considered a Muslim from Jakarta where he attended a Muslim school

Jim in Indonesia on Elephant Safari

from 1967 until 1971. When I pointed out that Obama stated that he is Christian, my new guide friend smiled and retorted that Muslims are encouraged to lie to infidels.

Chapter 13

Close Calls

I have had a few close calls during my early years. When I was about ten years old, I found myself being swept away by a raging river while swimming south of Calgary with friends. The undercurrent kept pulling me under, and, just as I was about to run out of oxygen, an angel disguised as a big, overweight man pulled me out of the water as apparently I went by him and he said, "What's the matter, kid? Forgot how to swim?"

At age nineteen, I drove my 1966 Chevelle into a rare traffic circle in Calgary and was clipped in the rear by a vehicle in the intersection. The damage was minor. Then, at age twenty-two, I was struck on the driver's side of my 1966 Chevy Station Wagon while idling at a red light. The damage was more severe, and while I was unharmed, I was covered in glass and shaken up some. In about 1978, at age twenty-eight, I was traveling through an intersection (I had the right-of-way) in my new 1978 Olds Station Wagon, and, unbelievably, I happened to glance to my right at that intersection and saw a vehicle driving at high speed that was obviously not going to stop at the stop sign.

I quickly hit my brakes, and I barely struck the rear side of that vehicle as it crossed in front of me at a speed estimated by police to be about fifty miles per hour. There were no skid marks on the vehicle that I hit. Think about that miracle for a moment. I was traveling about thirty miles per hour, hit my brakes, and was still moving ahead when I struck a vehicle crossing my path at about fifty miles per hour. Can you see the difference in time between that vehicle hitting me or me hitting that vehicle? It had to be a millisecond of time, and it me start to realize that God was walking with me, because he was not finished with me.

The vehicle that I hit was spun up into the air by the collision and landed nose down on the far corner of the intersection and in the grass landscaping. I can see it in my mind to this day. It was like slow motion. I could not get out of my car (which was totaled by the collision) because the collision had folded up the front of the vehicle like an accordion. Fortunately, I was wearing a seat belt and so was my passenger, and we only suffered severe bruising.

The steering wheel ended up in my chest, and my knees were on the dashboard. The driver of the other vehicle was also relatively unharmed. He ran over to our vehicle, asked us if we were hurt, and apologized for not noticing the stop sign. How many close calls have you had in your own life? Most of the time we take them for granted, or the momentary excitement wears off, and they go unnoticed.

I also loved motorbikes and had my final ride while moto-crossing through the wooded hills in Calgary at about age twenty-five. Dean, my sister's husband, had two cross-country motorbikes and asked me to follow him through the forest and hills. Unfortunately, he meant that I should follow him on the exact trail he was on, and I missed a turn while going downhill. It was bike, me, bike, me, bike, me . . . All the way down the hill to the bottom at about thirty miles per hour. When I finally came to a stop, with the bike on top of me, I slowly wiggled my fingers, then my elbows, then my shoulders and so on, until I was sure that nothing was broken. As painful as it felt, my body survived, and that was my final ride in an open, two-wheel motor bike that was not attached to a Disney World Ride or the like.

At age fifteen I was a tall, lean athlete (6'2 3/4" tall and weighing 145 pounds), but Barry Morris was much stronger. He could grab around a steel-basement-telescoping-support column and hold himself out parallel with the concrete floor for several seconds. His father had bought a brand new Ford. In those days, vehicle weight was massive, but so were the engines. I arrived at Barry's home, as planned on a warm summer evening, about midnight. Jumping into the vehicle, we headed for Priddis Road south of Calgary, to see how fast the new Ford could go.

The telephone poles were a blur as the car hit 120 miles per hour, and then Highway 2 suddenly appeared in front of us. We blew through the T intersection of the highway and through the ditch and then the barb wired fence and into the wheat field before coming to a stop. There were no seat belts that I can remember back in those days. I braced myself on the dashboard for what I thought would be my demise. Had there been any other traffic on Highway 2 that morning, the results could have been much worse than the scratches and front-end damage to that beautiful new car. I am not sure how Barry explained the damage. I was simply a bystander along for the ride.

The only other close call that I know of happened in Houston shortly after I moved there in 1981. I was awakened in the middle of the night by what sounded like a freight train passing overhead. I ran out into the front yard and looked up into the sky, quickly realizing that being out in the open was probably not a good idea. That tornado was hopping through our neighborhood, and it bounced over our home and into the adjacent golf course, where it caused significant damage to a number of majestic trees on the course. There was a very large oak tree at the end of our street, and all that remained after the tornado was a lonely, twisted trunk about fifteen feet tall, with no limbs.

Auntie Isobel and children with spouses

Uncle Bob and Aunt Cheryl with children and spouse

Nephew Brian and Christie with children

Cousin Cathy and Chris with children

Auntie Connie and Uncle Clay with children

Cousin Dave and Edie with children

Cousin John and Cathy with children

Granddaughter Kerry and Geoff

Nephew Kevin and Sarah

Steven, Peter, Heather, and Daniel

Heather, Brian, Kevin, and Peter

Cousin Tom and Laurie with children

Uncle Ken and Aunt Isobel with children

Sister Trisha with children and spouses

Chapter 14

US Citizenship

Upon receiving my U.S. citizenship in 1992 in a memorable ceremony, along with over 100 other new citizens from around the world, I went immediately to the Denton County Courthouse to get my voter's registration card and then to City Hall in Highland Village, Texas, where I still live, to volunteer my services as a new citizen. I was told that the only immediate possibility was to run for the Highland Village City Council, so I did so, and I won.

The story behind the story was that I entered the United States from Canada in 1980, courtesy of a temporary work visa obtained by my employer after advertising for the position and finding no qualified U.S. residents seeking the lowly oilfield position in the Williston Basin area of North Dakota, where the official state tree is a telephone pole. My immigration attorney recommended that I apply for a resident alien card, often called a "green card." That was great advice, because my temporary work permit expired just as my number was called up for immigration into the United States. My employer in Ray, North Dakota, and then Sidney, Montana, was Spartan Drilling of Calgary, Canada. My work visa had about a year left on it when I was employed there as general manager responsible for all operations of a branch with three oil well drilling rigs and four work-over rigs. Spartan Drilling assumed control of a bankrupt company through an agreement with the lender and key suppliers. The existing office manager had much difficulty with Spartan Drilling's takeover because he was part-owner of the bankrupt company. He apparently believed that I was an undocumented immigrant because he reported me to the border patrol, just a few short miles away. He was shocked when I was able to produce my work visa to the border agent, who had made a surprise visit to check me out.

Now, once Sherry (born in Beeville, Texas) and I married in Houston in 1987, I could have immediately been granted U.S. citizenship. However, I wished to complete my ten-year wait, holding my resident alien status, and then apply for citizenship. That is the normal process for those that hold a resident alien card, which is commonly known as green card. You wait ten years before you can vote.

It is my opinion that the U.S. government should build a southern border fence (the oceans serve as east and west borders and Canada is not an issue) around the United States. We all build fences around our home, so why not build one around our country, grant resident alien status to those that work illegally in our country, as long as they have worked and contributed without criminal status, then put them on that same ten-year wait before they can become U.S. citizens and vote. Democrats won't like my opinion because they look upon undocumented immigrants as voters and not people. Democrats seek power over people and want to trap undocumented immigrants in their oppressive system instead of liberating them onto the path of freedom.

Getting back to my election as a city councilman, I really didn't do much to win that seat and was fishing in Corpus Christi on the day of the election. In fact, I caught a trophy trout, and our guide took me into town to get my photo with the trout and to get it mounted. I have only had my picture on the front page of a newspaper three times in my life. The last two were on the same day. On the day of the election, I was featured on the front page of the *Port Aransas Gazette* with my trophy trout and on the front page of the *Lewisville News* as a new city council member.

I would like to forget the first time I was on a front page, but here it is. My Uncle Bob was just two years older than I, and he loved to be involved socially with just about anybody. He was about twenty years old when I received a phone call late one evening from a friend who was with Bob at a local Calgary restaurant, where we all hung out. He explained that Uncle Bob was very drunk and that the restaurant had called the police to have him removed. Being the thoughtful and helpful nephew that I was, I immediately jumped into my car and raced down Elbow Drive to rescue my uncle before the cops got there.

Unfortunately, the police that were headed to the restaurant clocked me traveling at a dangerous speed, and I was arrested (outside that same restaurant where my uncle was) and charged with dangerous driving, which meant jail time until I was bailed out by my parents. As I sat in the back of that police car after my arrest, Uncle Bob staggered over in a drunken stupor and asked me what happened and why I was arrested. The police were cracking down on young drivers, and my picture on the front page of the *Calgary Herald* the next day was the evidence of the crackdown for other young drivers to take note. I can think of other more enjoyable ways to be an example to others today, and I highly recommend them.

Chapter 15

The Baltic Region

Our family DNA points toward the Baltic region as the origin of our ancestors, so my brother, Peter, and I took a Baltic Sea cruise with guided stops and tours at the many countries in Europe that comprise the Baltic region, including Finland, Germany, Sweden, Latvia, Russia, Estonia, Poland, Denmark, and Lithuania.

We traveled by bullet train from St. Petersburg to Moscow, and the highlight was lunch on Red Square at the Kremlin. Our guide took us into the adjacent mall, which would equal any American mall, and then through hallways to the restaurant in Red Square, which was closed to the public but open to her friends. There we ate alone on an outdoor patio overlooking Red Square, the Kremlin, and armed soldiers, who were ready to pounce on us should the need arise. The underground subway system in Moscow is quite advanced, but the city itself is dreary and ordinary, for the most part. We found Russians to be quite stoic and quick to anger. Our guide made it clear that she would leave if she could.

In fact, our guide in St. Petersburg had that same complaint. We became Facebook friends, and, two years later, she realized her dream of leaving Russia after having married a gentleman from Germany, who then took her to Singapore, where they still reside. I let her know that I would be traveling to Singapore, and I got to meet her, her husband, and her new son, and she guided me around Singapore when I visited. The highlight was the Marina Bay Hotel, with three towers and a huge bar and a swimming pool across the top. She instructed me how to bypass security and to get to the roof, for guests only, at sunset, for one of the most special photographic opportunities of my life.

Peter and I also visited the Stutthof concentration camp in Poland and learned about the horrors of the war while looking at starvation menus and living conditions firsthand. Our guide's father was a tailor, and he was allowed to go home once a year in return for making custom German uniforms for the Nazis. She was the result of one of those yearly visits home.

There are three things for certain in this life. They are death, taxes, and change. The prisoners at that concentration camp, who were mostly Jewish but could be anyone that the Nazi's came to dislike, were fed a diet that would result in a slow, painful death in about six months, so death was likely forthcoming. They obviously didn't have to worry about taxation. That was the least of their concerns. That left change, and I suspect that hope for change was all that the prisoners could hang onto. Hope for an end to the war, hope for an escape, or hope for just about any change, because that couldn't help being an improvement for them. Even death, I am sure, would be a welcome change in many instances.

Change is inevitable. So life should be lived in the moment, especially when joy, peace, and prosperity are experienced. Change must be embraced and looked upon as an opportunity for more joy, peace, and prosperity. Discovering and recognizing your blessings and appreciating your lot in life is easy to say when thinking back on

Jim and Peter at the Brandenburg Gate at the Berlin Wall

Jim at the Kremlin in Moscow, Russia

Jim and Peter at Saint Basils's Cathedral on Red Square, Moscow

the prisoners of the Stutthof concentration camp. I wonder how hope could be held in the midst of all the misery. However, I'm certain that many held it. Joy in that environment would be difficult to discover and experience. Peace would be felt for only small amounts of time between beatings and abuse. And prosperity might only be felt when clean shirts or new shoes were provided. Or an extra helping of stale bread to eat. I can't fully embrace the circumstances of those poor souls, and these thoughts certainly make it easy to appreciate my life and to be grateful to God for my many, many blessings (https://youtu.be/U8DvvIlBTLQ).

Chapter 16

Alaska

I have been to Alaska twice. Our family cruise up the British Columbia coast could barely be called an Alaskan cruise, but it was an enjoyable time, featuring dog sledding on top of a glacier after a helicopter trip up the mountain. The coast of B.C. is considered a tropical forest supported by warm ocean currents from California, which cool considerably once they hit northern Alaska, and then these cold ocean currents head south past Japan. The same type of warm ocean currents come up from Africa to the United Kingdom, and, once they hit Greenland and the warmth has been lost, the cold water heads south past Newfoundland.

My second trip to Alaska happened with Joe Smith and three friends of his from Virginia. Charlie had liver cancer, and it was all he could do to board the small seaplane for our trip into Clark Lake near Mount Redoubt, which is a volcano. There, we had the most amazing day of our lives. Joe said that we could never have such an experience again, should we return with the others. The temperature was about seventy degrees, there was no wind, and we caught fish left and right and cooked them for lunch on the shore. There were eagles and bear everywhere, and the peacefulness was hard to describe. I will always remember Charlie lying face up on the bottom of our boat and declaring that he was in heaven, a place that he now lives after his lengthy battle with cancer.

We fished all over the Kenai Peninsula of Alaska during that week, and we experienced nature as you must experience it to enjoy it truly. Long walks through the woods to hidden streams and boat rides to remote, mountainous villages and to glaciers with walrus and seals made the trip unique (https://youtu.be/nwC1Ms6TvzU).

Sherry, Jim, Luke, Josh, and Marissa dogsledding on glacier in Alaska

Joe Smith and Jim fishing with friends at Lake Clark near Redoubt Volcano in Alaska

Chapter 17

Israel and Egypt

Israel is a special place. It's amazing that so much if it is way below the sea level of the Mediterranean, so if an earthquake were to strike at the continental divide between Africa and Asia, where Israel is located, it's possible that most of Israel would be under water, with King Herod's Palace at Masada barely above that new shoreline. Was that by accident? I think not. There are two seas along that continental divide in Israel. One is the Sea of Galilee, where many fish, plants, and other sea creatures live. I have sailed the Sea of Galilee with my brother and over thirty other Christians.

Our church service on that boat floating in the Sea of Galilee was yet another treasured life experience, of which we had many in Israel. The Dead Sea is located downstream near Masada, and it is toxic and dangerous. It is impossible to sink into the waters of the Dead Sea because of its extreme chemical-produced buoyancy, and the mud of that sea is purported to be a skin-wellness product, which is sold at the stores located there. Peter swam in the Dead Sea, but I only waded into it, after feeling the tingling sensation of the slippery, greasy-feeling water. He also covered himself with the mud from the bottom, while I photographed and videotaped this action, hoping he wouldn't die. This sea is also shrinking in size and appears to be disappearing into the continental divide. The Jordan River feeds it, but the Dead Sea is located where the water flow from the Sea of Galilee stops. No water visually leaves the Dead Sea, and, from the top of Masada, you can clearly see that the Dead Sea has shrunk into two seas joined by a small stream.

So why is one sea so different from the other? The Sea of Galilee receives water, and then the water flows out of the sea and becomes the Jordan River. The Dead Sea, on the other hand, receives water from the Jordan River but gives nothing back. The Sea of Galilee thrives and supports life because it receives and gives, while the Dead Sea only receives. That is an important life lesson. We flourish and experience all that life offers when we receive from others and then give to others in proportion. We die inside when we only take and do not give.

Visits to Jacobs Well, the David and Goliath battlefield, the Wailing Wall, and many other biblical sites were very impactful and served to bring the Bible to life for me.

Originally, Peter and I had planned to travel with a group to Egypt after our Israel journey, but, because of terrorism threats, that part of our trip was cancelled. After much discussion, we decided that we would be already in Egypt pretty soon and would not likely return again, so we sought out and found private tour guides for our Egyptian journey.

Flying to Egypt from Tel Aviv was an experience. There were no direct flights for the rather short journey. We flew out over the Mediterranean Sea and then back to Jordan, where an extensive series of security checks were undertaken upon our arrival. From there, we flew to Cairo and an unbelievable airport experience, where everyone, it seemed, was attempting to steal our bags. With much relief, we met our guide, who quickly made it clear to all the strangers around us that we were with him. The hotel was very luxurious. When we walked outside after breakfast the next day, we found ourselves in the shade of the great pyramids.

I asked Peter to take a photograph of me on a camel, with the pyramids in the background. With a serious shortage of visitors, the competition for our business in the camel herd was viscous. After I dismounted and started back to the hotel, I had a look at the photo that Peter took, and the pyramids were in the picture, but only part of the camel and just my head were in the picture. He explained that there was trash on the ground and he didn't want that in the picture. He was correct about the garbage everywhere. The government services were shut down, and garbage collection was a thing of the past.

Jim texting while driving in Egypt

Peter swimming in the Dead Sea

Jim at the Pyramids of Giza near Cairo, Egypt

Jim and Peter with Egyptian family at Cairo Museum

So we returned to the camel owners and negotiated yet another camel ride for me, along with a full photograph complete with empty plastic water bottles.

Our guide took us to the Egyptian market, where we were treated to a very good meal in an outdoor restaurant. Our guide was obviously highly regarded because the restaurant owner ran off some customers so that we could have some privacy.

She took us to the museum in Cairo, where a young couple kept motioning us and trying to communicate. Our guide was about to tell them to go away, when I asked her what they wanted. She replied that they wanted to have me hold their baby so that they could take a photograph. I told her that I didn't mind, and they were very grateful for the picture.

The highlight of our trip was a cruise down the Nile River toward Africa. The ship had just a dozen guests but space for at least 120 people. We were therefore treated like kings. The weather was great, and the view of the Egyptian shoreline was educational. Just beyond the lush, green vegetation and many homes lined up along the shore was nothing but sand dunes.

We visited many temples and museums, including the Jewish synagogue, where, according to our guide, Mary and Joseph hid with Jesus when they escaped to Egypt.

The only disappointment of the trip was the train ride back to Cairo. I would not recommend that as a means of travel through Egypt. I could not identify the food, and the smell from the restrooms was not pleasant.

Part of our tour was conducted by a fabulous Muslim guide, who had a great sense of humor and who was highly educated. His wife was a dermatologist, and they were planning to start a family in a couple of years after saving money to buy a home. Muslims are not allowed to borrow money, so they needed a large sum of cash to build a home. I asked him how his wife avoided getting pregnant, given the absence of birth control. He looked at me with a curious grin and replied that, like Americans, they both used birth control. That caught me by surprise. I then asked him if his wife covered her head when she worked. He responded that covering the body or head in any way was a family decision and that she dressed like Americans. I saw that firsthand later that day when three teenage girls passed us on the street. One in full-head-and-body robe, one with just her head covered, and one dressed like an American teenager. Our guide said that women often liked to cover themselves to avoid the wandering eyes of men (https://youtu.be/RbvE4eYJ14s).

Chapter 18

Equality

We come into this world depending on others; then we learn to be independent; then (hopefully) we learn to be interdependent. Jupiter is huge compared to Earth, but we depend on it to use its massive gravity to attract large and dangerous asteroids and meteors that would easily strike and severely damage our Earth if it wasn't for its presence. That is just one small example of how God, our creator, designed our solar system for our protection, and most of us are not taught these things in school. We are interdependent as a human species, whether we like it or not. Our very survival depends on it.

Striving for equality among ourselves is good. Striving for equal results is bad. It's just as simple as that. I felt as if I had worked just as hard as a medical doctor and that our opportunities were equal. However, he or she made different choices than I and was therefore paid far more than what I earned. Was that fair? Of course, it was. And if I produced more than what a peer did at work, should I be paid more? Of course, I should, and if my employer did not pay me more, I would be free to leave for an employer who would pay me what I feel that I am worth. Free. That is the key word. Free people are not equal. Equal people are not free.

Labor Unions do not offer freedom. As a Union member, you will become a number, labeled according to your years of service. Extra productivity is not only ignored; it is also often discouraged, because it makes your peers look bad.

Chapter 19

Your Gifts

The world has a place for all, no matter what your talents and God-given gifts are. And you are all blessed in different ways when you follow God. Those blessings might not be what you expect. God says he expects much from those whom he blesses. The more you receive, the more you should give—just like the Sea of Galilee.

You should always strive to be the best version of yourself rather than a second-class version of someone else. Have you ever looked at another person and wished you could be that person instead of you? The chances are that if you were in their shoes, you might think differently. Your God-given gifts and talents are not earned or learned. They are gifts that you are born with. Discovering those gifts is the thing. For me, I learned early on that certain people would make me uncomfortable.

There was just something that made me more aware of things when I was around them. Over the years, I have seen that such people have proven to be worthy of my caution and suspicion. It is called discernment. On the other hand, I have known people that I am very attracted to in a studious manner and that have proven over the years to be worthy of my attention and my desire to be friends with them. That is also called discernment. The Bible teaches us that it is our job to discern and God's job to judge, so I try to keep that difference in mind and basically avoid the bad dudes.

You are you because of your gifts, your heart, your abilities, your personality, and your experiences. The combination of these things will bring interest and passion and hope. When you find that certain activities or other things bring you joy and peace, you are likely experiencing that gift which God gave you and that makes you different from others. After all, if we all liked to do the same things, there would be much less accomplishment in our world. The result from there will be a change in your behavior. You will find yourself being compassionate toward others, humble in your demeanor, patient about all things, meek and kind, as you discover the joy, peace, and hope that God promises us.

You will also start to look at life's disappointments and tragedies differently. In a weird way, they become opportunities. My friend, Dale, use to tell people that if they dropped me in a barn full of manure, I would quickly start looking for the pony—and find it.

Chapter 20

People, Leaders, and the Future

There are three kinds of people in our world according to the movie and the memoir *American Sniper*, and I agree that our world consists of sheep, sheepdogs, and wolves. We need sheep. Lots of sheep. They are the ones that do all the work and that are often the happiest and most family-oriented folks that you have ever met. However, they are also easily led, and that can be good or bad, depending on the values of the one doing the leading.

There are many wolves in sheep's clothing out there, and sometimes they pretend to be sheepdogs, but they are not. Then some sheepdogs watch over and protect the sheep. They often give of themselves in secret, and they prefer to remain anonymous. They are strong yet silent, and they can spot a wolf, even those wolves dressed as sheep, from a mile away. They make great leaders, if they have the gift of leadership. They likely have a concealed gun permit and will risk their lives to protect others.

The wolves suck the very joy out of life. They are everywhere, and they enjoy misery. They persecute others through hatred, exclusion, insult, and rejection. It is amazing how they can attract sheep, who follow them, in spite of the misery that they inflict on others. Nothing that you say or do is good enough, and the wolves comment on the smallest flaw or imperfection. They are toxic personalities, and I run away as fast as I can from such individuals. Many of the wolves are very talented at concealing the full extent of their evil to their followers, and they often speak quite eloquently.

Now, as I learned to educate myself and to think for myself, I have found that there exist many puzzling and confusing political facts in existence in our country. We have, as a country of free people (so far, but that freedom is eroding), been electing and following those that seem intent on staying in power by promising free stuff and driving up our national debt to the point where, I believe, we shall never recover. That may sound worse than it is, but I do believe that the real pain is yet to come.

Endurance builds character. Our youth, if they suffer through years of reset of our world, will be bright enough to recognize the cause and will strive to get back to the basics that made our country great. For example, a return to the planting of vegetable gardens and living without advanced electronics may be in the works. Learning how to walk to work may become a necessity. Barter may be the new world order. Whatever we face, I am certain that we will overcome, with God's help and his assurance of a better life. I also am constantly amazed by our youth and feel confident that they will overcome whatever comes along.

Some of the things that I don't get are the result of a propaganda narrative that is constantly being fed to the sheep. For example, liberal political leaders accuse America of being capitalistic and greedy; yet more than half of the American population gratefully receive government handouts. Yes, the tipping point has been reached, and, from where I stand, the government appears like a wheelbarrow front-loaded and ready to tip over suddenly.

Our people are led by liberal political leaders to believe that they are victims of capitalism. And if such people join resistance organizations and go out on the streets and rebel and protest (and destroy the very small businesses that provide employment) and continue to vote for Democrats, will things will get better? Their Democratic representatives have been in power for most of the last ten years. Why would things get better? The poor are getting poorer, and the rich are getting richer? Food stamps are at a record high. Youth and minority unemployment are at the highest it had been for forty years.

That being said, the official poverty level in the United States as of January 1, 2017, for a family of four, $24,600, would be considered wealthy in much of the world. Our poor have cars, cell phones, medical care, and flat screens. When you have met a family, as I have, that lives in a one-room hut, sleeps on the ground on blankets, eats once a day, has no wardrobes, and is lucky to own a cow or goat, you realize just how (financially) fortunate that we are. Perhaps we need to return to more of the basics, and it is my guess that we will have no choice in the matter when the reset happens upon us.

A crab fisherman was once asked why he didn't put a lid on the bucket that held his day's catch. He replied, "The moment one of them climbs out, the others reach up and pull it back down again." We do the same thing, don't we? You come back down here with the rest of us! How dare you succeed? How dare you do well?

The apostle Paul warned, "But if you bite and devour one another, beware lest you be consumed by one another!" (Galatians 5:15).

You can not lift up another unless you are on higher ground. Seek equality of opportunity, and run from those that seek equality of results. This world needs quiet, humble leaders that have found that peaceful place in life, where they can silently help others without fanfare. Never quit your pursuit of that place. It is there, if you seek first the Kingdom of God.

The rich are not those that have the most. The rich are those that need the least.

Chapter 21

Technology

I remember working for Spartan Drilling in Houston in 1984 and receiving my first cell phone mounted in the trunk of my company car (a 1983 diesel Oldsmobile) with a handset on the front floor. It was so exciting to be one of the very first recipients of a cell phone. I loved that car, and it was years later (1991), after I was promoted by Space Master (in Dallas) to the position of vice president and general manager that I was asked to upgrade to a newer car to be an example to other employees and to reflect my stature of a senior position within the company. Of course, the large auto allowance did help, and my new red convertible indicated that I was now older than forty years of age and struggling with that fact.

In 1985, I purchased one of the very first Mac computers (Apple IIe) so that Sherry could continue her effort to complete her psychology thesis and spend more time with me than on her typewriter. That did not quite work out that way, but it was the thought that counted. Right? Sherry was attending the University of Houston full time and getting ready for the doctoral program. I was raising three teenagers alone after a recent divorce from Judy, and so we had little time together as it was.

In 1986, I received one of the very first fax machines, where I was working at Space Master in Houston. Each transmission of a single page took only six minutes. Wow, that was amazing, and I felt relief because our business was now able to provide same-day service.

In 1987, I bought an IBM computer to replace an aging, memory typewriter and earned the distinction of being the first Space Master branch office that converted many menial tasks to the computer.

These remarkable advances in technology were just thirty years ago. Imagine where we would be now without computers and cell phones. Imagine where we could be now if the Obama presidency had stepped out of the way of job creators, thereby liberating the creativity that was within them and helping them to really advance our technology. Obama had his foot firmly planted on the throat of our economy for eight years with his (mostly) illegal regulatory overreach.

Chapter 22

Entrepreneurship

"Success is the ability to go from one failure to another with no loss of enthusiasm."

—Winston Churchill

"The enemy of mastery is the belief that greatness already exists."

—Tony Jeary (https://youtu.be/SvqytzZf2aQ)

My first venture into the world of controlling my own time and using my experience for personal gain came while I was employed at A1 Camp Service in Edmonton. I had left Atco Structures after ten years of employment and joined a start-up oilfield camp catering supplier owned by Brent Elton. He and Guy Turcotte approached me at the Oilfield Show in Calgary and offered me a sales position with the potential for stock ownership. The company grew rapidly in a strong economy. Two of my customers asked me to help find vendors who could provide specialty products and services over a winter camp season (December–March). One customer needed generators and electrical harnessing for four seismic camps, supporting forty–fifty people. The other needed movie entertainment for the manpower in ten drill camps. Brent declined to provide these services to our customers, but he said that I could do so if I wanted.

I formed JASS (James Attrell Sales and Service) and used my industry knowledge to locate suppliers and vendors who could support my new business. VCR was brand new technology (imagine that!), and very few people owned the new recording device. I found a service center that built plywood boxes with handles that contained a nineteen-inch color television (massive in size at that time) and a VCR tape machine with a fan and a long power cord. Hollywood was on strike at that time, and the television stations were playing old movies, which I recorded to VCR tape on slow play. That way, I was able to put three movies on each tape. Those tapes did include normal television advertising, but remote camp personnel couldn't be picky. I rented each box from the service center over four months at prices that fully paid for the equipment, which was returned after the lease was fulfilled.

That coincided with the winter drilling program. I volunteered to deliver to one of the camps set up near Fort McMurray in northern Alberta. Unfortunately, I broke my glasses the day I was to deliver the goods and was forced to wear my prescription sunglasses, but the delivery was slated to occur in the middle of the night, which required driving on winter roads created by plows as access to winter oilfield projects. These roads existed only in the winter.

The drive was about six hours north of Edmonton. The plows would keep the snow removed down to hard-packed ice on a regular basis, throwing the fresh snow on either side of the road to four feet or more in height. So there I was in my station wagon with emergency fuel, water, and other supplies, trucking along at about seventy miles per hour on the fairly straight and lonely ice freeway when the road suddenly took a sharp right turn. All I could do was hang on tight, as my car jumped the snow bank and plunged into the forest. In northern Alberta, those forests consisted of small evergreen trees that rooted down to the permafrost that never melted. Keeping my foot on the gas pedal was essential in order to prevent getting stuck in the snow.

As I ran over trees left and right, I turned the car around so that I would hit the snow bank and arrive back onto the road. That worked great, except that I hit the snowbank head-on and my momentum put my car through the road and over the snowbank on the other side of the road. Not losing my composure, I once again gunned the gas pedal, as I tore up the forest again, and turned the car around, this time at an successful angle to the snow bank. It was unbelievable how little damage I had done to my car that night. There had been no traffic on the road. The rest of the trip went fine, including my return trip that same night, because I had to be at work the next day. To fully appreciate a blessing, you must experience hardship.

My hardship that night might not seem like much, but I did feel very blessed when I returned home safely in my warm car. Deuteronomy 31:6 says: "Be strong and bold; have no fear or dread of them, because it is the Lord your God who goes with you; he will not fail you or forsake you." After that very busy winter-drilling and exploration season, the federal Liberal Party government in Ottawa announced that it was nationalizing the oil industry. The new regulations resulted in the immediate departure of drilling activity by the large multinational oil companies. Unemployment and business failure skyrocketed. A-1 Camp Service pretty much shut down business operations in Canada and started operations in Texas. Our best customer in Texas was Spartan Drilling, out of Calgary, and I would soon go to work for them in North Dakota, when A-1 Camp Service ceased operations.

Chapter 23

Challenge and Opportunity

In 1995, I left Space Master Buildings after ten years of employment to join John Transue of Advanced Modular Space as a contract salesperson sharing in the profit of each sale. Unfortunately, that system meant that I did all the work for less than half the profit, so I set out on my own, with Jerry Brown as my partner, and sharing accounting cost with Mike Mount of Indicom Buildings, a major supplier. The new company was Modular Space Corporation, and we opened a new office in Flower Mound, Texas. Business was tough.

When it became apparent that our relationship with Indicom was in danger and that we were fast running out of money, I left the business to Jerry and went to work for MPA Modular in Arlington, Texas. The company offered a good salary and ownership in a new leasing operation that I built over a year. The owner, it turned out, was trying to sell the leasing business behind my back. Of course, I relied on trust, not thinking that having a signed agreement might be a good idea. I immediately left and went back to work for Space Master in Carrollton, Texas. The owner informed me (confidentially) that the business was in the process of being sold. He essentially warned me that I was value-added to the sale price of his business and that I would need to be prepared for the event.

When Sherry and I formed Nortex Modular Space in 1998 (while I was employed at Space Master), it was a choice between unemployment, being moved to California, or starting a new business. I recognized that, with the merger of the two largest modular building companies in America (Space Master and Williams Scotsman), there would be a significant opportunity for a local Texas-based small business that served the custom marketplace. We sold one automobile,

Nortex Factory and Employees, Lewisville, Texas

cut back on expenses, and started our new enterprise at a small desk in the family room of our home. And, of course, we had a small Apple computer.

I learned quickly that banks would not loan to a new business, but I was fortunate that a new community bank in our neighborhood was staffed with a loan officer who was a friend and a fellow church member. Jerrell Jenkins was a constant mentor and suggested that I take advantage of the new law introduced by then-Governor George Bush, allowing us to take out a second mortgage of $65,000.00 on our home to capitalize the business.

Jerrell pointed out that, after we displayed a period of success, we could use the capital as collateral on loan to grow our business. It became quickly apparent that banks do not take much risk. Jerrell provided a step-by-step process in line with how I wanted to develop and grow a custom mobile- and modular-building leasing business and to tap into government needs for energy-efficient housing for office and classroom use.

When we won our first lease contract, while remembering that the $65,000.00 at the bank was untouchable, I purchased the building from a large competitor and paid for it in cash from an advance on my Master Card. After several months of proven history and with the $65,000.00 still in the bank, Jerrell helped us to obtain an SBA loan.

The rest is history, and our incredible success must be attributed to God's bringing us the best employees at the right times. We grew to over 1,000 building units in our lease fleet, $30 million in annual revenue, and 100 employees at the peak in 2009, when we sold the business to Black Diamond Group in Calgary, Canada. What I remember most is paying off 100 percent of our corporate and personal debt and withdrawing the original capital investment of $65,000.00.

We were able to establish a donor-assisted charitable foundation to support our church and favorite charities and family trust accounts to support and educate our family members.

About that time, along with Jay and Bettye Rodgers and David Hammer (who helped us immensely in the sale of Nortex to Black Diamond) we formed Biz Owners Ed (BOE) (https://youtu.be/yrOYdZGgo4M), a nonprofit organization that trains and develops successful business owners. Of course, the sale of Nortex and that we were creating a business-training organization that might be dangerous to the election of Democrats, we were audited by the IRS, and nonprofit status for BOE was denied. The IRS audit took about a year, and the net result was zero impact, except for $30,000.00 in legal expenses.

Our BOE attorney wrote Lois Lerner at the IRS and suggested that her opinion concerning our nonprofit status was not legal. Of course, we did receive our nonprofit status eventually, and although we had no intention of political activity, the approval arrived well past any date when we could have been effective politically. Lois Lerner asserted that we could only be a nonprofit organization if we educated only minorities. Not wanting to attract negative attention, we decided not to participate in the later investigation of Lois Lerner and her politically motivated and illegal activities at the IRS.

About this time, Gary Lewis at United Community Bank asked me to serve on the bank's board in an advisory capacity. Learning about banking from the inside was an experience—especially after the 2008 financial collapse, caused in large part by Democratic politicians making it, as an example of the atrocity, easy for unemployed individuals to buy a home absent a down payment. Of course, that was done in hand-holding with Wall Street, which packaged up such loans and sold them to unsuspecting investors. Make a point of watching the movie The Big Short (https://youtu.be/jl3KSg4l9gM) which accurately portrays the financial collapse or our banking systems. Congress was warned about the impending disaster a number of times by conservative leaders (https://youtu.be/cMnSp4qEXNM).

Democrats held party lines and voted to continue the insane practice of lending money to just about anyone with little or no down payment required.

As a result of the financial collapse, bank regulations were put in place that made it impossible for a smaller bank to survive because of the numbers of administrative report-writing employees that the government required. Our bank was fortunate to have a relatively small portfolio of bad real estate–related loans, and we were able to sell the repossessed property at a profit, in many cases, mostly because of our strong north Texas economy, led by a Republican government. However, it was apparent that, going forward, we needed to do what was best for private shareholders and sell the bank to a larger bank. It's sad that smaller community banks are unable to survive bank regulation.

From January 20, 2009 through January 19, 2017, it was hilarious to listen to Democratic politicians in Washington, D.C., explaining to their sheep that our economical problems would be solved if banks would start lending, when it is regulation by the federal government that prevents lending. For example, our bank could not offer a proven, long-term business customer a preferred interest rate unless that same preferred rate was offered to a business owned by a minority customer. The problem was that there were no minority-owned businesses that were seeking a loan.

Over the next few months, I was able to visit with several larger banks, soliciting bids on the purchase of our bank and obtaining the necessary nondisclosure agreements, and we were able to close that sale shortly after selecting the best offer. Of course, that larger bank already had the necessary regulatory personnel on staff, so our personnel were discharged. This was yet another example of job-killing government regulation.

While I was employed at Nortex (after the sale to Black Diamond), I purchased a small piece of commercial property adjacent to the Nortex property in the Riverview Industrial Park in Lewisville as an investment. With the help of our attorney, Pete Benenati, we formed Marluc, LLC to hold the property.

Later, after I retired from Nortex in 2011, I purchased a small two-bedroom house about two miles from home in Highland Village and set it up as an office under the Marluc, LLC corporation. Marluc then hired Dan Sarine, who had left Nortex, where he was the manager of accounting. Dan took care of accounting and managing our properties, and we started acquiring homes within a mile of our office (that was a rule) and renting them. Because we were paying cash, it was usually pretty certain that sellers would take less to ensure that a sale would close without issue. We quickly grew the business over the next three years to twenty-four properties. In 2016, we started selling properties as they came off lease and cut our holdings in half by the summer of 2017. Dan left Marluc early in 2017, and Marluc hired Jan Jenkins (Jerrell Jenkin's wife) on a contract basis to handle all accounting functions, and I took over property-management responsibilities. This became a challenge after a major hailstorm struck and destroyed the roofing of every one of our two dozen properties.

However, the good news was that we had great insurance coverage and that when we listed a home for sale, we would have at least ten offers within twenty-four hours, and many offers exceeded our asking price. When friends wondered why we were selling our homes in a hot market, I reminded myself that the time to sell was when it was too early. At the time of this writing, Black Diamond (the company that bought Nortex Modular Space) stock that was trading at $70.00 per share stock is now selling for less than $2.00 per share.

What I have learned through all my experiences as an entrepreneur is that fear is much stronger than greed. "It is fear that makes cowards of us all," said Vince Lombardi.

"Clarity, Focus and Execution are the three stool legs of a life of success."

—Tony Jeary

Chapter 24

The Antarctic

Where is the most beautiful place you've ever been? There are many magnificent corners of the Earth, and the Antarctic is one of them.

Jim's first steps on the Antarctic Shoreline

The Antarctic is an amazing place. As a photographer and videographer, I would not think that this is the place to go, but traveling with some of the best National Geographic photographers and world-renowned scientists on one of the world's largest icebreakers was an eye-opener. I could have done without the two-day Drake Passage crossing and its thirty-foot waves, and I can't imagine how explorers like Stapleton were able to cross the passage in much smaller boats.

We attempted to travel on the regularly scheduled route, going on the south side of the western peninsula, but, for the first time in modern history, it was iced-in during February, which is a summer month in the Antarctic. Daytime temperatures ranged from twenty-five to thirty-five degrees, and the sun never set. It was light at all times.

Our daytime routine was a morning trip to shore on inflatable boats after breakfast and coffee for three–four hours. Then, after lunch and a period of relaxation on the boat, we would return to shore once again for another three–four hours. The trips always included a trip to see penguin populations, and we also climbed a glacier for a spectacular view of the surroundings. We made many trips through colorful, floating glaciers and encountered whales, leopard seals, and many species of birds everywhere. Before departing from or returning

Jim overlooking the bow of the National
Geographic Explorer Icebreaker

Jim with a friendly penguin on the
Antarctic Shoreline

to our icebreaker, we were required to be disinfected to prevent any accidental transfer of undesirable virus, plant life, and the like.

At one point, I was taking a photograph of our ship on the horizon, nestled in the snow-capped mountains just as a humpback whale "fluked" in front of me. What an experience. The ship had a small submarine equipped with a video camera, and, every evening, the marine scientist on board would play the video from the day, outlining the names and types of the marine life species that were encountered. He explained that although it would get extremely cold above the surface, the temperature below the surface never was colder than about twenty-nine degrees and stayed there year-round.

The Antarctic contains over 80 percent of the world's fresh water and is the only place on Earth where the ice is growing in mass. The continent has, without the ice, the highest average altitude in the world and is easily larger than the United States in size. Unlike the Arctic, the Antarctic consists of significant land mass, whereas the Arctic has little land mass under the ice. The Antarctic is the windiest place and the driest place on Earth (https://youtu.be/isa9_gCH6do).

Chapter 25

Africa

Until I visited Africa, my trip to
the Antarctic was my favorite. My
Africa trip started with a flight to
London. I caught a taxicab and
drove to Godstone, Surrey, where
my grandfather, Stephen Attrell,
was born. I asked a local resident
about the address of his birth, and
he said it was not an address but
an actual home. Coincidentally
(another miracle), it was across the
street, and as I photographed it,
a truck pulled up, and the driver
asked me what I was doing. When I

Jim on walking safari in Botswana,
Africa

explained, he jumped out and said he was the owner (another miracle)
and lived there, and he summarized to me the long history of the
home. It was here that Grandpa lived until he was six years old, when
the family moved to Alberta.

After traveling from Johannesburg, South Africa, to the "Cradle
of Humankind" (for Darwin fans) about sixty miles away, I flew to
the Mala Mala private game reserve adjacent to the Kruger Game
Reserve, where, for three days, I experienced the most excitement
and adventure that you can imagine. Every day included an amazing
close encounter with every form of major wildlife that exists in Africa.
The accommodations were luxurious and safe, although I could see
elephants and antelope from my patio door. We were escorted to and
from our individual small homes, and we were waited on hand and
foot. We traveled off-road in open jeeps with a guide and a large caliber
gun. Our guide had worked there for years and had never had to use

that gun because (it became quickly apparent) the animals recognized and respected his presence. On the first day, we went to a sandbar on the river, where two hyena packs were fighting over their kill while the buzzards ate their fill. For over an hour, we parked right in the middle of that event just a few yards away and in an open jeep. The next day, we heard that lions had killed a young cape buffalo, and when we arrived, two males were devouring it while two lionesses looked on.

We parked in our open jeep, just thirty feet away from the male lions, and watched as the cape buffalo herd attacked the lions. The largest male lion finally took off with the kill in his jaws and passed me by mere feet as he ran into the bush. We followed him into the bush and watched in amazement, as the buffalo charged the male lion, causing him to abandon the kill.

After approaching the baby buffalo and realizing that it was dead, the mother started to leave. The rest of the herd also left. The female lions (who caught the baby buffalo in the first place) tried to retrieve the kill, but they were quickly chased off once again by the mother who, once she realized she was alone, took off toward the herd. The female lions then ran to the kill, but they got only a few bites before the male lions took over the picnic. This whole event lasted about forty-five minutes, and I carefully photographed and videotaped the entire event.

I saw and photographed, from a short distance, cheetahs, elephants, alligators, hippos, tigers, lions, giraffes, rhinoceroses, snakes, wild dogs, warthogs, and birds of all kinds—just to name a few.

I then traveled to the Mashuta private game camp in Botswana, where I experienced more of the same and a guided walking safari through the bush. The guides were armed and experienced at tracking wildlife for photography, and I filled my camera with some really great shots.

Next, I flew to the Xakanaxa Camp, where I lived in an above-ground tent and traveled the rivers looking at the wildlife. At night, I could hear all sorts of large animals walking around my tent and inspecting my presence, but I was assured that no harm would be forthcoming.

My final experience occurred at Victoria Falls, one of the largest falls in the world, and that trip included a helicopter flight over the falls. I also visited a local village in Zambia and learned how trade with other villages support their economies. Like Haitians, the people had little in the way of possessions, but the village was organized and led well by individuals who understood that trade, productivity, and responsibility were important to the well-being of their community. Every child and adult had a job to do, serving others. Two of the youth were in a makeshift jail that resembled an open bus stop with a barbed wire door. One of the mothers was openly chastising the boys, who apparently had gotten drunk at a nearby village and had been returned to this village, where they lived. It is law in Zambia to carry identification, and Christianity (apparently) was Zambia's form of government. If you could not identify yourself, you were taken

Jim at Victoria Falls in Zambia and Zimbabwe, Africa

to the border and told not to return. Immigration was not a factor because it was discouraged. There was a church on the corner of almost every intersection in Gambian villages, towns, and cities, and the people were pleasant, humble, and helpful (https://youtu.be/IzZWk8ZCrnc).

Chapter 26

Japan

I have visited Japan twice. The first time was a bucket-list trip to see Mount Fuji. I purchased a rail pass in the United States before I left because rail passes are not available in Japan. The special aspect of that trip was that my friend, Jim Sloan, was the American Airlines captain on the flight and that we enjoyed some time together before his return flight. Jim is now battling prostate cancer, and Robyn, his wife, has retired so that they can spend lots of time together.

I was able to travel to Tokyo and onto Mount Fuji only because the Japanese are so darned helpful. They always went out of their way to be of assistance, and I very much enjoyed the journey, although it was cloudy and rainy upon arrival. I took photos of postcards showing a sunny mountain retreat and sent them home by Facebook, acknowledging that the photos were not mine. Tokyo itself was very clean and could easily be mistaken for any modern city in America. I very much enjoyed watching the people shopping, dining, and visiting with friends. They have an amazing park, with lots of familyadventure opportunities.

My second visit to Japan occurred because of an upcoming shortfall of Executive Platinum miles on American Airlines. My concierge suggested that I fly there and back first class, with a three-hour layover, and because of a promotion, I would get double miles and a discounted fare. In exchange, I received eight system-wide upgrades, allowing me to make future international flights in the first class section. Nice. I also received an Admiral Club membership and the usual perks provided to Executive Platinum customers.

When I arrived at the Dallas-Fort Worth airport for departure to Narita, Japan, I discovered that I had my passport but had left my wallet containing my cash and credit cards at home. The American

Airlines desk clerk said that I had all I needed for the long flight and that because I was traveling first class and staying at the American Airlines Admiral Club during my three-hour layover, I would not need cash, credit cards, or additional identification during my twenty-eight-hour absence from home. That was another miracle, I believe.

Chapter 27

Hong Kong

Hong Kong was a one-night layover while I was returning from my last trip to China. I didn't have much time, but I spent what I had by walking around one of the downtown areas. The Starbucks took my iPhone app for payment, and I knew there and then that all would be good. The Social Security system there makes a lot of sense, as explained by my driver.

He said that as long as he worked, a portion of his paycheck went into a government bond fund, which paid his account a small amount of interest, with the capital used to finance the construction of public projects. Upon his retirement, he could cash in his account and invest it as he pleased, or he could take out an annuity good for the rest of his life, with interest, on the basis of how much he had paid in.

If only our government could come up with a similar plan for our retirement. We save money, and the government uses it to build infrastructure, such as highways, bridges, and airports, and pays us a guaranteed interest rate and return, and we cash it in when we retire. We keep what we earn, and the government does not have to sell treasury bonds to foreign countries.

Chapter 28

India

My journey to India was certainly one of my most spiritual, as I traveled with my friend and international speaker and corporate evangelist Krish Dhanam. (malaministries.org)

Jim and Krish Dhanam at Taj Mahal in India

We visited Krish's parents and the Taj Mahal, with many stops along the way to fulfill Krish's extensive preaching and speaking engagements. I saw Krish do the most amazing things and remember fondly the sound of his flip-flops across the hotel room floors early every morning as he prepared for each day. Sitting in the front row of a crowded Assembly of God Church in Chennai, I saw him preach to a congregation of several thousand and a television audience with far-reaching impact (https://youtu.be/kL5TSPNG8o8). But watching him flawlessly tape four five-minute mini-sermons in a radio station without a break was astonishing.

During a presentation at a business school and a discussion on morality, Krish surprised me and invited me to the stage to answer a question from the audience. The young college student stated that an employee of her family business was stealing from the company, and she asked what I thought she should do. I responded that the company, hopefully, had a written set of expected employee standards so that they could immediately fire that thief. She responded that the thief was her brother. I was speechless and remembered that almost every business in India was a small family business.

Krish had coached me that I was safe in India but that I should not leave anything of value lying around, because it would be stolen.

Jim and Krish training students at the CMT Business College in Visakhapatnam, India

Like many places in our world, rightful possession is 90 percent of the law. Krish also preached at a large Methodist church in Chennai, and the communion ritual is just like that of Trietsch Memorial Methodist Church in Flower Mound, Texas, where we have our home, except that you take off your shoes and leave them at your pew.

We visited the Taj Mahal after a very long four-hour taxicab drive through the rural areas of India. Watching a troop of wild monkeys walking down the roadway was a first for me, as was much of what I saw. Even more exciting was crossing roadway intersections where the rule is first-come, first-serve, and all drivers or pedestrians think that they are first (https://youtu.be/OwuYyYDSHMM).

Trisha, Uncle Bob, Kim, Jim, and Peter

Family Reunion and Mom and Dad's Home

Grandma Attrell with visiting family members

Grandma Attrell with sisters

Grandma Attrell, Christine, Dad, Trisha, and Mom

Kim, Jim, Doreen, Auntie Audrey, and Peter

Jim, Peter, Mom, and Trisha

Grandma Attrell, Kim, Cathy, Trisha, Paul, Jane, and Thomas

Trisha and Jim in Calgary at family home in Southwood

Auntie Connie and Uncle Clay with Clay's parents and children

Chapter 29

Retirement

I awoke one night (fifteen months after we sold our business) and could not sleep. I had a stomach ache, just thinking about going to work at Nortex Modular Space. I no longer owned the company and had sixteen months remaining in a thirty-six-month earnest-money contract.

My responsibilities were significantly reduced, and the veiled promise of "no change" was quickly forgotten. I was consulted, but pretty much ignored. The success of the past seemed meaningless, and new people were brought in to manage functions that they did not understand. I protested, but to no avail, and I left by announcing my retirement.

It cost me two years of earn-out cash, but, in the end, it boiled down to how much money was enough money.

And with the direction the company was heading, my third-year earn out was significantly at risk anyhow. I left on good terms, and, through Biz Owners Ed, our nonprofit training and mentoring organization, I can now enlighten others on my experience. David Hammer, my friend and my professional advisor, told me that a three-year earn out was not usually completed after the sale. I should have listened to the experienced words of the wise. However, I proudly left with the check marks all on my side of the ledger. That's how it should be. Otherwise, regret would have been like a cancer in my system. Besides, I felt an obligation to my ex-employees to leave things in outstanding condition.

My retirement party was awesome and another very special memory with all our employees, major vendors and suppliers, and friends in attendance. I'd like to repeat that gathering regularly and experiencing that level of friendship daily is awesome. I do get to lunch and fish and do other activities with my friends regularly, and, to this

date, I will always want it to be that way, as long as I am breathing.
There are so many good memories jam-packed into our twelve years
at Nortex Modular Space. I feel that we were able to touch many lives
positively.

I did wish that Jeff McClain could have been there. Jeff was
instrumental in our entry into manufacturing our own buildings, and
if it wasn't for Jeff (who died from a cancerous brain tumor), we might
not have been the nation's leading manufacturer of energy-efficient
green buildings. Jeff worked hard, and I feel good that, because of
our benefits package, his family was able to pay his medical expenses
and buy a new home with the life insurance payment. It was sad to
watch Jeff visit us in our factory while struggling with his illness and
experiencing his desire to help us when his ability to speak was gone.
He would draw on paper to express his thoughts. Thank you, Jeff, for
all that you did.

I do have one regret, and that involved illegal immigration. We
used a third-party payroll service to make certain that we operated
legally in every way and that we could provide employee benefits. That
brought us to a level of professionalism that many small businesses
could not achieve. However, at one point, the high cost of health
insurance forced us to seek another more competitive health insurance
provider, who required our employees to be treated as brand-new
employees under all the new employment laws.

We realized that some of our factory workers might be found
to have provided falsified documentation when we originally hired
them, but we never imagined that thirty-five of them (one-third of
our workforce) could not provide the necessary paperwork to continue
employment. Many of these individuals were not just employees. A
bond of friendship and appreciation had been formed, and, looking
back, I don't believe that, knowing what I know now, we would have
changed third-party agencies.

That being said, the factory is no longer operating (the new owners
shut it down), so it was God's will that these employees returned to
their homeland in Mexico, where the economy is now much improved.
I do regret that we could not pay them a bonus for their service. They
were asked to provide proof of valid Social Security numbers within
two weeks; then they simply did not show up for work. Our factory
workforce was suddenly cut in half. At least when we later laid off
workers because of work shortages, I was able to shake their hands,
thank them for their service, and say good-bye.

That work shortage occurred after we had sold the business and
liberal antibusiness policies started to take hold. The new owners were
a publicly traded (Wall Street) business entity and, therefore, they had

no interest in providing anything more than what the law required of them. Once again, you will hear me say this often: big is not better!

The most important lesson I learned at Nortex was that when you leave things to go wrong, they will go wrong. I practiced management by walking around. Talking to employees about their jobs was not only enlightening and interesting; it also helped me to stay in touch with the people who counted most in our organization. I always made certain that all employees understood our mission statement and that they were free to speak about it anytime and anywhere if they thought others were ignoring any elements of our mission.

Chapter 30

Peru and the Amazon

Traveling to Peru and the Amazon with my sister was a real treat. I take seven minutes to get ready to go after I awake, and she takes about forty-five minutes, but we made that work.

One of the most enjoyable parts of the trip was a luxury train ride up to Machu Picchu and back. The food and entertainment were excellent, and it made our two–three hours at the peak most enjoyable. Our ship on the Amazon had twelve rooms, and Patsy and I took up two of those rooms. The crew tied the ship up on the shore every night after dark, and, for the most part, we hung out during the evening and traveling hours on the open top deck beside the bar, enjoying the cool night air over an adult beverage.

Jim and Trisha at Machu Picchu in Peru

Donkey at 12,000 feet altitude in Peru

We spent a lot of time exploring the jungles and visiting villages along the way. Our guides were natives from these villages that had attended college and had been hired by National Geographic for these scientific excursions paid for by the travelers. Patsy got to swim with the dolphins, and we made daily motorized boat excursions to the most fascinating places. One day, we encountered thousands of large, white-winged birds (like pelicans) that flew up from the river in front

Jim and Trisha in Amazon Village

of us and then flew beside us, as we raced up the river waterways. It was pretty exhilarating. On the last day of our adventure, we dined in a beautiful beach-side seafood restaurant in Lima, Peru, at sunset and enjoyed the conclusion of a fabulous adventure (https://youtu.be/86jH0GmSb04).

Chapter 31

Spain

One of my favorite cruising experiences took place with over thirty friends to Spain and Lisbon, Portugal. Lisbon is a beautiful city, with much history and great tourist spots. The cruise was organized by Jay and Bettye Rodgers, who have made this an annual event for their friends. It is unfortunate to see countries such as Spain undergo such horrible economic issues with high unemployment and youth leaving the country, seeking a better life elsewhere. Spain's economic issues are an excellent example of how debt related to Socialist policies and giveaway programs will eventually ruin a civilization.

We stopped at different ports every day, including Guernsey in the English Channel. The weather was great, and the fellowship and friendship of my travel mates is a fond memory. There is nothing equal to waking up every day with family and friends at your side. We were not meant to be alone, and the lifelong transition from dependence to independence and then finally to interdependence can be shortened by sheer will, and I highly recommend it.

After arriving at Lisbon, I left for home, and the rest of the group sailed across the ocean for another week to Florida. I have a basic need to put my feet on good old terra firma every day, and the thought of traveling across the ocean, even with friends, was not the least bit enticing. Call me a landlubber. That is what I am (https://youtu.be/Dvq_yDcfrMg).

Chapter 32

Turkey and the Danube

My favorite trip with Jay and Bettye and friends, including graduate students from our BOE annual classes, started in Venice, Italy, with a cruise to Istanbul. This was my second time riding a gondola through Venice, and both were suburb experiences. Besides stops in Greece, we made a stop at Ephesus along the way and got to visit the place that was once was one of the largest cities in the world and the final home of Mary, mother of Jesus. Paul wrote in the Bible about converting Jews to Christianity from the coliseum located here, and we visited that

Jay and Bettye Rodgers with Jim and Friends at Ephesus in Turkey

facility, as well.

After our arrival in Turkey, we flew to Budapest in Hungary, where we boarded a riverboat cruise ship and traveled through Austria and Slovakia to Germany and then onto Munich. We stopped every day for a land tour, and the weather was ideal. The scenery was often breathtaking, with many great photo opportunities. In Munich, I attended Octoberfest and the village where the Israeli athletes were murdered during the 1972 Winter Olympics. My cab driver knew exactly where we were going when I gave him the address and remembered vividly the terrorist attack on the Israeli athletes (https:// youtu.be/oUn8iNUTgKs).

Chapter 33

Italy

My first visit to Italy happened during the 2006 Winter Olympics, with my friend, David Tedesco. After a tour of his father's birthplace and a visit to Rome, where we visited such famous places as the Vatican and the Coliseum, we met a friend of his and had dinner on the rooftop of City Hall, overlooking the many famous sights located there. His friend was the City Hall janitor, and his employer provided him with a small rooftop apartment in exchange for his services. He shopped the food markets during the day for table scraps and cooked for himself. We dined on shark-jawbone meat cooked with pasta, and it was fabulous. The train was our favorite method of travel. When we approached Pisa, David arranged for a taxicab to take me to the leaning tower just long enough to take photos and say that I was there. The officials in Pisa no longer allowed climbers, so my two-minute visit worked just fine.

Sherry, Luke, Jim and Marissa in Florence, Italy

David and Jim at the coliseum in Rome

Marissa in Florence, Italy

We traveled by train to Saviango, where a friend provided us with a home for the week that we attended the Olympics The venue was located not far away from Turino. David and Ted Meyer joined us there, and the highlight

Luke at the Eiffel Tower in France

was the gold medal hockey game between Finland and Sweden. David and I made several side trips, including one to Monte Carlo for a little gambling (that lasted for about fifteen minutes). We also went to Lake Como to see David's friends there. Everywhere we traveled, we spent time with David's family and friends. On one occasion, I spent the entire evening dining and drinking homemade wine, with a full dining room of his distant family, and they only spoke Italian. They carried Grandma down the hall to join us, and she smiled and laughed the entire evening, but she never spoke a word. That's the Italian Social Security system. You take care of your own.

David died recently after succumbing to a cancerous brain tumor, and he is missed terribly. Travel has a way of bonding people and lives. If you ever have the opportunity to travel with friends or family all together, do it. You won't regret it.

Chapter 34

111

During the last ten years or so, I have noticed many times where the numbers 11 and 111 have become prevalent during my normal day. This onslaught usually stops abruptly after a couple of days. As an example, I was visiting my son, Tim, in Columbus, Ohio, about ten years ago, when I first noticed these strange messages (and that's what it felt like—messages).

My hotel room was room number 111. When I asked Tim about the restaurant where we were meeting, he told me the street number of the address was 111. I glanced at the clock when I got to bed that night, and it was 11:11. Certain that there had to be some meaning to this development, I searched the Internet, and, sure enough, I was not alone. It seems that this happens to many people, or enough people, that it has drawn much attention and study. The so-called experts say that the universe (I think they mean God) is speaking to me or that guardian angels are letting me know that all is well. I have many, many examples of what happens over the course of a day or two. Once, I was watching CNBC on television when I was interrupted by a phone call. I hit the pause button, and, after completing my phone call, I looked at the paused TV screen, and the Dow Jones was trading at 11,111.11. What are the chances of my hitting the pause button on my remote control at that exact moment in time?

I have awakened a few times in the middle of the night at exactly 1:11 am. I have been given restaurant bills for $11.11. As I said, these coincidences will go on for a day or two and then stop for months. While I am not superstitious, I really believe that there is a message here, so I am going with the guardian-angel thought.

I also don't believe in fortune tellers or psychics, but I did consult, by telephone, with a psychic named Sammy twice in two–three years. I even recorded the conversation for future reference during the second call, because, during the first call, she said that she saw me coaching a young son at soccer, but my two sons were grown, and there was no new son in the foreseeable future. Well, along came Luke in March of 1993. Intrigued, I called her back, but, so far, she has been off the mark in her predictions. I am pretty convinced that only God knows what is coming, so I, for one, will be saving my money and avoiding future temptations to try to know what the future is bringing.

The point is that you just never know. You never know what's going to happen in life, and mysteries abound!

Chapter 35

Envy

There are two Americas. The America that works, and the America that doesn't. The America that contributes, and the America that doesn't. It's not the haves and the have-nots; it's those that do and those that don't.

Some people do their duty as Americans: they do obey the law, do support themselves, and do contribute to society. Other people don't do their duty as Americans: they don't obey the law, don't support themselves, and don't contribute to society. That's the divide in America. It's not about income inequality; it's about civic irresponsibility. It's about those that preach hatred, greed, and victimization. It's about the love of power more than the love of country.

The politics of envy commonly note that some people make more money than other people and that some people have higher incomes than others, and believers in such politics say that the difference is not just. That is the rationale of thievery. The other guy has it; you want it; and envious politicians will take it for you. That is the philosophy that produced Detroit. It is the electoral philosophy that is destroying America. It conceals a fundamental deviation from American values and common sense, because it ends up not benefiting the people who support it, but a betrayal of those people.

Liberal leaders have not empowered their followers; they have enslaved them in a culture of dependence and entitlement, of victimhood and anger, instead of ability and hope. You cannot reduce income inequality by debasing the successful, and you cannot seek to deny the successful the consequences of their choices, and you cannot spare the unsuccessful the consequences of their choices. Why? Because, by and large, income variations in society are a result of different choices leading to different consequences.

Those who choose wisely and responsibly have a far greater likelihood of success, while those who choose foolishly and irresponsibly have a far greater likelihood of failure. Success and failure usually manifest themselves in personal and family income. You choose to drop out of high school or to skip college—and you are apt to have a different outcome than someone who gets a diploma and pushes on with purposeful education. You have your children out of wedlock, and life is apt to take one course; you have children within a marriage, and life is apt to take another course. Most often in life, our destination is determined by the course we take.

It is a false philosophy to say that one man's success comes about unavoidably as the result of another man's victimization. Liberal leaders foment division and strife, pitting one set of Americans against another for their own political benefit. These two Americas are coming closer each day to proving the truth to Lincoln's maxim that a house divided against itself cannot stand. It's all about envy.

Chapter 36

Health

"Never go to a doctor whose office plants have died."

—Erma Bombeck

Stay connected, stay active, eat well, help others, get help, take care of your soul. As time moves on, the speed at which it passes intensifies. In October 2010, I made my first iPhone notes entry that my weight was 251 pounds. I felt fat and unhealthy.

My chiropractor of several years (I still see Dr. Martz every month) introduced me to a blood type diet to help me learn how to eat healthily and lose weight. The nutritionist who wrote the book about this diet also offered an iPhone app that helped me to focus on the super foods and avoid the unhealthy choices—all on the basis of my blood type, O. It's funny, but I had a heck of a time trying to find out my blood type. I couldn't give blood because of my Leiden Factor V blood disorder, and so I had to pay for a test. Following that diet, I gradually dropped to 198 pounds in February 2013. So I lost fifty three pounds over twenty eight months. I was not exercising in any way, other than walking regularly during my world travels. Since then, I have fluctuated between 200 and 215 pounds, mostly because of relative inactivity.

Leiden Factor V is an inherited blood disorder that causes the blood to clot much faster than normal. As a child, I would get a nose bleed after a vicious football hit, but my nose would stop bleeding very quickly. An accidental deep cut in my hand would bleed for just seconds. Little did I know that, some forty years later, I would get a blood clot in both legs after a long car trip followed by a long airplane trip.

The doctors diagnosed my disorder, and, from that point forward and for the rest of my life, I have taken and will be taking (daily)

warfarin, a blood thinner commonly used to poison rats. I received
this medical gift from my mother and had shared it with (at least) my
daughter, Marissa. Of my five children, the odds are that two–three
of them will test positive for Leiden Factor V and that half of their
children will test positive. The good news is that there are no known
side effects to warfarin medication and that my blood system is not
likely to get clogged up again.

My only other serious health issue was a bout with polymyalgia
rheumatica, which was a painful arthritis condition impacting my
hips and shoulders to the point where I needed help to get dressed.
We never did determine the cause, but my chiropractor feels that my
immune system was harmed by all the vaccinations I had during my
travels. Of course, these vaccinations, such as the ones for hepatitis
and tetanus, were given to me to ensure that I didn't return home with
some strange disease. All I know is that I woke up one day after my trip
to Argentina and the Antarctic and that my hips were painful. Then
my shoulders. After suffering through several weeks of severe pain,
I was referred to Dr. Penmatcha, a rheumatologist who immediately
diagnosed my condition. He prescribed prednisone, and the relief was
immediate. Unfortunately, the drug has many side effects (I was fine),
so he gradually reduced my dose over eighteen months to zero, but the
disease then returned with a vengeance, so I was forced to start all over
again. After twelve months I was once again pain-free and remain so to
this day.

There was a Texaco gas station near my Calgary home in
Southwood. In later years, I would work at this gas station, but when I
was a twelve-year-old, the wavy steel fence presented a tight-rope-type
walking challenge. The result was a wicked gash below my right shin.
Knowing that Doc Medlicott was my likely destination had I reported
the injury to my mother, I attempted to care for it myself.

By the time she noticed my blood-soaked pants, it was too late for
stitches, which pleased me immensely. Forty years later, I would be
diagnosed with squamous cell carcinoma (skin cancer) at the scar. The
doctors offered a type of surgery, where they systematically removed
a layer of skin and then tested that skin for cancer, while I sat in the
waiting room with numerous other skin cancer patients with obvious
major skin cancer issues. When told that the test came back positive,
I went back into surgery, where the surgeons removed and tested yet
another layer. I asked the surgeons what would happen if they kept
taking layers down to shin bone without success, and they said that I
shouldn't think about that possibility. "Thanks a lot," I said, not feeling
very comforted.

Finally, after a day spent mostly in the waiting room, the surgeons informed me that the last surgery was successful. It has been about two years since that happy day, and my old scar is now a bigger scar. I guess I should have told my mother about my metal-fence injury at the Texaco station a little earlier. I still remember myself as a ten-year-old running full tilt into the framework of a wooden fence in a new subdivision. Doc Medlicott put twelve stitches in what was left of my right eyebrow. In those days, you were not provided with any type of painkiller. Dad called Doc, and he met us at his office near our home. He would always remind me that I would be a big boy if I held still while he stitched me up. Those dozen stitches went in very quickly. Dad gave him $10.00, and we were done. There was no such thing as Canadian government-funded health care insurance in those days, and that $10.00 was not tax-deductible. A good monthly paycheck in those days was about $250.00. I guess you can see why I was hesitant to report my shin injury to my parents.

When they first introduced national single-payer health care insurance in Canada, I was a young father about to have our first child (a daughter). I was nineteen years old and earning $350.00 per month, and it was a welcome program. The monthly deduction from my paycheck was very tiny, compared to the cost of having two more children (sons) over the next three years.

Regular free trips to the hospital became the norm, and, over time, the monthly deduction by Alberta Health Care increased as my income increased. I look back and am grateful now that I know that high-income earners paid for my health care through higher and higher income taxation. I thought the Canadian government paid for my health care, not knowing that the government got its money from taxation on the population. I thought they just printed those Canadian dollars. Don't get me started. I had the privilege of being seated with the British Columbia minister of health at an Olympic hockey game in Vancouver in 2010. My new employer (who had purchased our business, Nortex Modular Space) was Black Diamond Group of Calgary, Canada, and it had a suite at the hockey game. What I learned was that the cost of health care in British Columbia was out of control and that the minister was going into retirement, feeling like a failure. He watched as government-funded health care insurance became an entitlement program with unbelievable abuse encouraged by labor unions and protected by the legal system. As a percentage of the British Columbia budget, free health care insurance went from less than 10 percent to 35 percent, and rising quickly. Everyone, it seemed, was "on the take" and liked things just as they were.

I took a slap shot off my ankle during a hockey game in about 1976 at the Fairview Community Center in Calgary, where I was also the sports director. As a defenseman, you are trained to directly face an oncoming puck because your protective padding is all located on the front of your hockey equipment. However, it is natural in the heat of the battle to think you are invincible, and I quickly found out that I was not. The doctor said that I would need the cast for about six weeks. I asked him how the cast would be removed, and he explained that there would be protective gauze under the cast when it was sawed off.

During a fierce winter storm about a month later, I got a flat tire in front of my house in about twelve inches of fresh snow. After bringing my spare tire, wrench, and jack to the flat tire, I wrapped my left leg and right leg (with the cast) around the tire, jacked up the car, and removed the flat tire. However, I had forgotten to set the parking brake. Slowly the vehicle started rolling forward into the snow, and, by that time, I noticed my cast was firmly planted under the wheel, cushioned only by the snow. As my toes started to go numb, I quickly reset the jack and was able to jack up the car enough that I could remove my leg from under the wheel. The cast was bent into my shin. My toes were numb, and it wasn't because of the cold weather. I limped to the garage and sawed off the cast with my hacksaw. The relief was instant. It felt so good that I went ahead and played hockey that night, fully believing that I was healed enough and that my skate would serve as a cast on my ankle if I tightened the skates up beyond the norm. A month later, the doctor's office called, wondering why I had not returned to get the cast removed. Doctors cared about their patients in those days.

I played old-timers hockey in Fairview for two–three years on a line with Andre Castonguay, one of the very few French-Canadians that lived there. One night, Andre passed the puck from the corner to my awaiting stick, and I quickly snapped a shot at the goalie from the slot and scored. With my right skate firmly planted in the ice during the follow-through of my shot, one of the other team's defensemen delivered a hip check, which tore the cartilage in my knee. I underwent surgery and then rehabilitation over three–four months before I could play again. Years later, I was wrestling with my son, Tim, and I tore the cartilage in my left knee. That surgery was completed with a scope, and the recovery was much quicker.

However, I decided I didn't need rehabilitation, and, to this date, I am unable to bend my heel to my buttocks because of that poor decision on my part.

In fifth grade, my eyesight deteriorated. I had to borrow Rita Nelson's (a classmate's) eyeglasses in order to see the blackboard. For the next ten years, I relied on glasses. Then, the first contact lenses became available. The first ones were huge. In my forties, I underwent surgery to correct my shortsightedness. However, my close-up vision was a problem. So I still needed glasses in order to read. It turns out that almost everyone develops close-up reading vision difficulty in their forties. In 2010, I was one of the very first individuals that had HD lens replacement surgery which corrected both close-up and distance vision. However, the new lenses were pliable, which resulted in small hemorrhaging in my eyes, creating big floaters. My eye surgeon then removed the vitreous fluid in my eyes and replaced it during two separate surgeries. My vision is now almost perfect. I am so grateful for that gift. I can feel, smell, see, hear, and taste. What could be better than that? With just one of these senses, you can squeeze the juice out of life. With all five of these senses, we should be eternally grateful. If you could only choose one, which would you choose? Think about that for just a moment.

Actinic keratosis is a precancerous condition of the skin. Twice I have had treatments for the skin on my left cheekbone. Left without treatment, the skin becomes cancerous, resulting in some very serious surgery. Of course, without surgery, the result is death by unpleasant means. I encourage everyone to visit a dermatologist on a regular basis. It's a very quick and inexpensive process. During my last visit, my dermatologist looked at my forehead and determined from a biopsy of the skin that I had melanoma, a third type of skin cancer that I had not yet experienced. Once again, I underwent surgery, and today I have a nice forehead scar to remind me of the experience. At the suggestion of my doctor, I have since given up golfing as an alternative to plastering my skin with sunscreen and wearing long-sleeve shirts and pants in the hot sun.

In 1974, I was having difficulty swallowing food. The doctor said that, after years of acid reflux, my esophagus had become scarred and restricted. He recommended that I undergo surgery to repair a hiatus hernia condition. That surgery helped for a couple of years, but my difficulty continued. In 1979, I rushed myself to the hospital, unable to swallow food stuck in my throat or to throw it up. They put me under and removed the food. Later that year, I spent a night unable to sleep, with steak stuck in my throat and unable to get it either up or down. The doctor showed me how to relax, loosen my belt, and get the food down. What a relief. Surgery to remove the scarring and to enlarge my esophagus helped again for a few years, but my difficulty swallowing food continued until I discovered that I was gluten intolerant and that therefore wheat products caused acid reflux.

I have seen my chiropractor, Michelle Martz, on a regular basis since 2002. My first visit was to seek relief from a hip pain, which she quickly diagnosed after a thorough examination of my physical condition and my spinal X-ray. As a hockey player, I preferred skating to the left. My tie always hung to the left. It turned out that my left leg is shorter than my right leg by three-quarters of an inch. That had caused my spine to lock and my hip to tip to one side. I remember bending over at work (after several treatments) and feeling my spine move.

I called Michelle, and she assured me that my spine was supposed to move freely. Imagine that. It took several months and heel lifts in my shoes for the pain to go away, but it did, and I have been free from discomfort for several years. My monthly visits have become maintenance visits, but because I have no pain, Medicare does not cover the cost. Some would suggest that I report pain, but I couldn't live with that lie. For most of my life, I could not stretch my right arm above my head without pain. Michelle indicated that my shoulder was slightly out of joint, and she adjusted it immediately so that I no longer experienced that discomfort. Finally, I was never able to turn my head left and right to the extent that I can now. That problem seems minor, but I was thrilled to know that there was more to my physical ability than what I thought there was. You will never know what you are missing until you discover what you are capable of doing. You all have hidden talents that will surface over time if you stretch yourself into unknown territories on a regular basis. Squeeze that juice out of life. Amaze yourself. We all come into this world in the same way, but we leave in many different ways. How will you leave? It will have much to do with your health.

Chapter 37

Bankruptcy

Challenges and disappointments are a natural bump in the road.

One of my more impactful bumps was bankruptcy. I moved my family to Houston from Sydney, Montana, in 1982, while working for Spartan Drilling, Inc., a subsidiary of a Canadian oil well–drilling contractor. The oil industry was in the midst of a severe downturn, and my task as vice president of Marketing was to land day-work and footage contracts with quality oil companies at survival rates. I landed new contracts with Shell and Exxon that would have done just that, but we drilled a very expensive and very deep dry-hole for a small operator in Oklahoma, who went into bankruptcy and did not pay us.

The result for us was bankruptcy, as well. In 1984, I was given a choice to return to Calgary and work for Spartan Drilling in a contract capacity or to remain unemployed in Houston. Judy and I had separated, leaving me to be the primary caregiver of our three teenagers: Jennifer, Chris, and Tim. After our divorce, I met Sherry and fell in love with her. She was in graduate school at the University of Houston, and we met through a new dating service that I had signed up for. I was not about to leave Houston.

Unfortunately, my divorce and poor financial situation created a great hardship on my children. Jennifer went into a severe depression and became addicted to drugs. Fortunately, my health insurance at Spartan Drilling was still in place, and it covered her intensive hospital treatment for about a year. When I was unable to pay medical expenses beyond that year, she was discharged, and I was told that I was responsible for about $250,000.00 in doctor and hospital bills.

After several failed part-time commissioned sales positions in an economy with a 12 percent unemployment rate, I landed a job and a new start on life with Space Master Buildings. Fortunately, my resident alien (green card) status had been approved. However, with so many unpaid bills and no financial resources, my car was repossessed while I was at work.

That was one of the most embarrassing experiences of my life. Sherry had a CD at the bank and borrowed from it to fund the purchase and repair of my 1983 Oldsmobile, which had been parked for quite some time. The phone calls from creditors were becoming more and more of a problem. And when they found out that I was working, they started calling me at work. It was obvious that I would not, in the foreseeable future, be in a position to repay and fulfill my financial obligations, so, with the help of a lawyer friend of Sherry's, I declared personal bankruptcy in 1986. I recently celebrated the thirtieth anniversary of that depressing event.

What's somewhat humorous is that American Express, after twenty years, forgave the debt I owed (it's actually the bankruptcy law that it do so) and issued me a new credit card that shows that I have been a customer since 1978. Bankruptcy in Houston during the economic downturn of the early 1980s was pretty common, but looking back, if my debtors could have left me alone with my promise to pay when I could, my preference would have been to choose that route instead, and I most certainly would have done so some five–six years later. The hospital and doctor bills, however, were a different matter. During the year that Jennifer was hospitalized, I think that the insurance company was "milked" by the hospital for everything that they could pay. The bills were excessive beyond belief, and when the insurance just stopped paying the bills and when I was unable to pay them, the hospital suddenly announced that Jennifer was cured and released her.

Chapter 38

The Great Flood

In 1988, Sherry and I bought a very nice home in the Houston community of Inverness Forest near FM1960 and I-45 and just south of Spring Creek for $63,000.00. The home had a history of minor flooding and was located just outside of the 100-year floodplain. Flood insurance was not required, but our decision to purchase it anyway had to be God-inspired, because we were poor. Our new home was close to my office and to Sherry's new job as a psychologist employed by a small, but growing, family-counseling business, and she was pregnant with Marissa. Shortly after we moved in, a tropical storm dropped fifteen inches of rain on our community in one night. Sherry woke me up in the middle of the night during the storm. I stepped onto the floor into six inches of water. Just a few short weeks prior to the storm, I had an Achilles heel operation, and I stepped into that water with a cast on my leg. Sherry was pregnant. She was very concerned about her maternity clothes, so I threw them onto Chris's water bed. Chris is my oldest son, and he was attending a local high school. Waterbeds float, and thus her clothing was safe.

We each picked up a dog and walked up the flooded street to a friend's home. We had anticipated a potential flood risk and parked our vehicles at high ground up the street. The next day we walked down to our home and found it to be under forty-four inches of water, confirmed later by the water markings inside and out. It took three days for the water to subside. That gave me time to prepare for the teardown and reconstruction of our badly flood-damaged home. My duties at Space Master included Project Management over my construction projects, so I was able to redirect subcontract construction personnel to my home to handle the expedited repair. I ordered a forty-yard dumpster, which could easily contain a large pickup truck.

Friends arrived, and they emptied our home of its contents that either went into storage in our garage or into the dumpster. Most went into the dumpster. I had won a new bedroom suite in a work-related sales contest, and it included a large, round mirror about five feet wide. The wood perimeter was obviously particle board, because it was swollen two–three times thicker than the part that did not get wet. A permanent watermark was on display, right across the middle of the mirror. I had become good friends with Dale Wheeler of Dal-Bar Construction, and he and his employees were a godsend during this time. We completed the rebuilding in just six weeks at a time when very few of the over 100 homes in our subdivision had even started repair. The insurance company inspected the repair (as did the city inspector) and paid the mortgage company. The mortgage company then inspected the work and reimbursed us by check. Sherry felt uncomfortable moving back in on that day, because another tropical storm was arriving, so we stayed another night at our temporary home with a friend, who was a flight attendant and gone much of the time.

Unbelievably, we found ourselves in the middle of another severe flooding. Sherry attempted to drive her Ford Taurus into the garage of our temporary home and found herself in about three feet of water at the bottom of the driveway. A neighbor rescued her and managed to push her flooded car up the driveway. Our just-repaired home, in the meantime, was under two feet of water. We were the only home in the Inverness Forest subdivision that would book a totally separate second flood claim. You might say that the second time that I rebuilt the home, the work was not completed with quite the same enthusiasm. I called my employer and expressed a strong interest in moving to any area of the country where Space Master had an open position. Dallas had an opening for a new branch manager, and I quickly agreed to the relocation.

Sherry and I moved into a townhouse near our flood-damaged home and prepared for the arrival of our daughter, Marissa, while I repaired our home and worked at Space Master. Again, I completed the work in a few weeks. My father was a real estate salesperson in Houston and sold our home the same day it was listed for more than we paid for it. Because of the quick sale, we were able to buy a new home in Highland Village in December 1989, just weeks after Marissa was born. A fresh start. With all of worldly possessions in a U-Haul trailer. A bed, a fridge, and a few boxes of photos. A new house, a new job, and a new baby. God is good.

Chapter 39

Flying Lessons

In 1977, I was working for Atco Structures in Calgary and the Contract Administration Department. This position was a tremendous learning ground, because I coordinated all activities of specific manufacturing and construction projects, from inception to conclusion. I worked at Atco during most of the 1970s. In 1977, the opportunity to work on some international projects developed, and I spent several months working in Houston and in the same office as my father (Doug), who had also worked for Atco in a senior sales capacity.

Dad had been transferred there from Calgary permanently to develop the international exposure of the organization. The company placed me in a corporate apartment with another Atco employee. He was a project manager and a Vietnam War veteran. One night, I heard gunfire by the apartment pool. I ran down the stairwell and peeked around the corner to see a man holding a gun pointed at a woman in the pool. My roommate raced past me toward the attacker, while I ran back to the room, displaying a basic fear of death and logical and protective behavior. More on that later.

My roommate returned shortly, wild-eyed and fired up. All he could say was, "Wow." From what I could gather from him, he struggled with the attacker and wrestled the firearm away from him just as the police arrived. He served on the "cleanup crew" in the battle zones during the Vietnam War and was terribly scarred by the experience. The company let me return home to Calgary every two weeks for a long weekend, but, after six months, I requested a return to full-time duty at home. My Houston boss had wanted me to transfer to Houston and the International Division, but I was very homesick and the hockey season was starting back in Canada. He was a pilot and loved gliders. I made one glider flight with him just west of Houston, and it prompted me to take flying lessons upon my return to Calgary—

at Springbank Airport. The weekend that I was to fly solo, I was
hospitalized with pneumonia.

Then I ran out of money to fund my newfound hobby. The
most harrowing experience was practicing takeoffs and landings by
performing "touch-and-goes." The approach fields alternated between
snow-covered farmers' fields in frozen, harvested crops and plowed,
black-loam fields. The snow-covered fields were cold and leaned toward
downdrafts while the clear-dirt fields leaned toward updrafts. Touch-
and-goes require maximum use of runways, and I hit a downdraft
while attempting to land at the beginning of the runway.

Had my instructor not hit the throttle hard when he did, I'm afraid
I wouldn't be writing this account today. The downdraft rattled my
teeth pretty good and came close to causing undercarriage damage to
the Cessna 150 that we were flying. Incipient spins were not my favorite
exercise. The instructor would make certain we had lots of altitude to
work with; then he would have me close my eyes while he put the plane
in a nosedive and then put it into a spin. The first time we did this,
my watch broke under the G-force pressure exerted upon it. My face
felt contorted, and it was hard to think, but today I am confident that
I could safely pull a plane out of such a dive. It's a little like curing a
life that is in a nosedive. First, you eliminate the power of the dive by
turning the throttle to minimum. In life, you would ignore everything
else that is going on and simply stop doing whatever it is that is the
cause of the problem.

Second, you turn the wheel just enough to eliminate the spin.
In life, you would rid yourself of any and all bad influences on the
direction you wanted to go. Third, you pull gradually back on the
wheel, bringing your nose up so that you are leveled up with the
horizon. In life, you look at where you want to go and make final
changes in preparation for the journey ahead. Finally, you hit the
throttle and turn toward your destination. That's when you know that
you have overcome. It's a sweet feeling and a most exhilarating one.

Life is like that, as well. Heading in the right direction at full
speed will always rule. Deuteronomy 31:6 tells us to be strong and
courageous. I call it "squeezing the juice out of life." A few years later,
I experienced my second close call while flying in a helicopter in an
unexpected snowstorm in northern British Columbia, while I was
employed at Atco.

The pilot quickly descended into a deep river valley so that he
could see. We were surrounded by rocky cliffs on either side of us.
I was so relieved when we finally came into sunshine after a lengthy
ride above a winding, white-water river. My third close call happened
in a chartered small plane in northern Alberta. I was working for A-1

Camp Service. The pilot was taking me to a small airstrip near an oil well–drilling site, where I was to meet our camp-catering staff. The pilot flew into a snowstorm, not knowing where it started and ended. He was also not familiar with the area. After an hour or two of a rocky flight, he decided to turn 180 degrees and fly back to the point where we had entered the storm, after he had calculated what direction the storm was headed, which was the direction that we had been heading. After we broke out into the sunshine with minimum fuel, I promised myself that I would not ever put myself at that potential risk again. I do have a basic fear of death. Since then, I have flown only on commercial airlines, except for a King Air twin-engine flight to Calgary from Houston, and helicopter trips with my family up to a glacier in Alaska to participate in dogsledding, and over Victoria Falls. It was fun to watch Sherry leading a dogsled in Alaska. Marissa holding dog sled puppies is also a fond memory.

Chapter 40

Hockey Season

I was captain of my Boy Scout hockey team in Calgary, and a photo of that bunch of young teenagers with Coach Bill Buzan proudly hangs in the men's restroom wall at our Ranch Lodge. I was always a hockey fan. I really didn't know anyone who wasn't. Hockey Night in Canada was 6:00 p.m. on Saturdays, when everything in Canada came to a

Captain Jim and Boy Scout Hockey Team

halt for three hours. There were just six teams in the NHL back then, and just two in Canada. It was hard to cheer for Montreal during a time when French Canadians were absent from western Canada, and most of my friends were Toronto Maple Leaf fans. I was a big fan of Guy Lafleur, who was affectionately known as "The Flower," but he played for Montreal. Every day I would open the newspaper sports page to see how many points Guy and his line-mates scored.

Canadians manned every position on every team, including the four U.S. teams in Detroit, New York, Boston, and Chicago. It wasn't until the late 1960s that players from elsewhere in the world started to compete for starting positions on NHL teams. When Bobby Hull was not selected to play internationally on the Canadian All-Star Team because he had joined a new league called the WHL (World Hockey League) that was competing with the NHL, he took out American citizenship and played for the U.S. team in the World Championships. That set the hockey world on fire. Fans were outraged. The WHL soon failed, and most of the teams joined the NHL in a much-needed expansion.

My team of choice was the Edmonton Oilers, who played 200 miles north of Calgary, where I lived. As a season-ticket holder, I drove to every game. I remember one Saturday night game that was played in the midst of a province-wide snowstorm. The RCMP had closed the highway from Calgary to Edmonton, but my father-in-law, Gus Sundell, and I convinced the

Dave, Howie, Dennis, Danielle, Randy, Jim, and Dave at NCAA Hockey Championship, Tampa, Florida

police that we had front wheel drive and chains, so we drove through snowdrifts several feet deep in places and arrived in time to see the game. After I pled to him for weeks, my manager at Atco Structures relented and transferred me to Spruce Grove, Alberta, so I could be close to my team.

I coached my kids at hockey during this time and left the Fairview Community in Calgary, where I was the community sports director of hockey teams comprising thirty-two kids and a beautiful new hockey arena. We lived across the street from the rink, where either I or one of our kids played a game or practiced almost every night during the work week or during the day on Saturdays. One of my fondest memories was merging our sports organization with that of three other communities that, like us, had declining youth populations. We had a rink, and they didn't. They had the financial resources, and we didn't. It was a simple solution and resulted in the formation of the Heritage Sports Association. Naturally, there were communities that we competed with that accused us of wanting to "load" our teams with good players. One of the perks was playing old-timers hockey twice a week in the rink late at night. In order to play, each person had to serve in a volunteer position at the rink.

My choice was driving the Zamboni machine, which scraped the ice clean and laid a new surface with hot water. The hot water made for a superior skating surface when it froze. Leaving this community was hard, but the challenge of a job change with better-earning opportunity, coupled with taking my kids to see the Edmonton Oilers play in my hometown, where I was born, was just too good to be true. I remember standing in the player's concourse before games with all my players' hockey sticks under my arm.

Wayne Gretzky was my favorite player, and he stopped and autographed every stick (https://youtu.be/RCrUcovi820). He was the best player ever in the entire world, and he was kind and thoughtful. It was he who said that "to succeed, you needed to skate to where the puck is going." He also is known for saying, "You will miss 100 percent of the shots that you don't take." That is so true in life, as well. I miss those cold winter nights flooding the outdoor hockey rinks. The skill of building a good rink that would last well into March during that time was important. Some of mine lasted into April. It was all about getting the soil wet and then frozen to a significant depth. After each period, the parents would climb over the boards with shovels and work in unison to scrape the ice clean for the next period or game. No one had to ask; it was just expected. I followed Wayne Gretzky wherever he played and generally cheered for whomever he played for. As years went by and I moved to Texas, I found myself coaching a tiny-mite team in Houston. In a city of millions, there were just thirty kids aged nine–ten that played hockey, and half of those were new to the game. The only teams that existed for us to play against were those in Dallas, Austin, and Oklahoma City.

The parents would pay for us to fly to these cities for a weekend tournament. I was in Dallas and had moved there when the Dallas Stars won the Stanley Cup in 1999. That was an exciting event for Texas, and hockey had grown in popularity ever since, with new rinks being built and new kids' teams being formed every day. My son, Luke, played for a year at an early age, and he got to meet Darian Hatcher, the all-star defenseman and the captain of the Dallas Stars. I met some like-minded hockey fans in our community and found myself joining with Randy Guttery, Dave and Dennis Casey, Howie Wright, and Dave Meyer and attending the NCAA College Hockey Championship (called the frozen four) every spring in whatever city it was held.

I have many fond memories of these trips. The same alumni from the various colleges and universities with hockey teams come every year, and we have made lots of new friends that we see just once a year for four days.

Often, the good seats to the games are hard to find, and hotels around the venue are quickly booked. I was slow to book a hotel room in Milwaukee one year and accepted the only other option, which was to bunk in with two of the guys, using a foldaway bed. Arriving late and after the office closed, I found that the foldaway bed was broken, and I spent the night in a V-shaped poor excuse for a bed.

Randy thought that was appropriate punishment for some of the practical jokes I had pulled on him. On one occasion, I found a beautiful, but deceased, hawk in a field near my home. Knowing that Randy was selling his home and had a couple coming that afternoon for a second viewing, I spread out the hawk's wings and carefully laid out the bird at his front doorstep. When he called me later to tell me that a hawk had slammed into his front door and died on the spot, I couldn't help laughing and revealing my guilt. He paid me back in excess by placing a gay-pride sticker on my truck's license plate, which I drove with for weeks before noticing other drivers' reactions as they drove past me.

To even the score, I booked airline seats for Randy and me on our next hockey trip and reserved a window seat for him right next to the jet engine.

I also have made a number of separate trips with my friends to places where the Dallas Stars play. I have collected a puck at each NHL arena where I've seen games, and I am now the proud owner of thirty NHL pucks from every single NHL rink in Canada and the United States. Dave Meyer and I have also attended the Winter Olympics in Italy and Vancouver. The highlight was the Gold Medal game between Sweden and Finland in 2006 in Turino, Italy. Yup, hockey is absolutely the most entertaining of all sports. When I was a child, we would play soccer, baseball, and football in the summer, and all we talked about was our winter hockey team—who the coach would be and who would be on our team. Game on!

Chapter 41

Smoking

My earliest memory of smoking was the day I smoked at my grandparent's farmhouse in the garage when I was about fourteen, with my Uncle Bob (two years older than I) and my cousin John (a year older than I). I quickly became addicted. I smoked plain cigarettes and cigarillos. Filters reduced the nicotine rush that I craved. By age nineteen, I was smoking about fifty cigarettes a day and drinking several bottles of Pepsi.

Between the heavy dose of nicotine, caffeine, and sugar, my body weight remained under 150 pounds for years, which was too little for my (almost) 6'3" height. The first and last thing I did every day was to smoke a cigarette. At work, I would light up a cigarette, using the one that I had just finished, thereby saving on matches. After a little bout with pneumonia and a subsequent review of my chest X-ray, I decided to quit smoking at about age twenty-eight. My physician explained to me that the craving for a cigarette that I felt when I did try to quit smoking was actually my "black" lungs trying to heal themselves. He also pointed to my X-ray and said that my lungs were about done and that I had the lungs of a very old man. That woke me up. My wife (Judy) and I decided to take a week-long vacation in the Bahamas with my goal to relax and quit smoking. I chewed on Bic plastic pens full-time and drank vodka straight-up to kill the desire for smoking. And when the desire became unbearable, I went to bed and slept. About a year later, I went to the bar with my friends from our adult baseball league. I didn't think that one cigarette would hurt, but it hooked me for about six months. Quitting the second time was even harder, but Judy agreed to quit smoking in our home and car to help me.

She would go outside into a snowstorm to smoke. After a few years, I discovered that broccoli actually had a taste, and, after about thirty years without a cigarette, my sense of smell has returned. I smell things now that I am not sure I have ever detected. It makes my love of the outdoors and nature much more enjoyable. I do need to avoid places like Hereford, Texas (with the largest stockyards in the world). Trying the eat a steak in a nice restaurant there is difficult when all you smell is cow manure. Another benefit of giving up smoking was the relief from circulatory problems. My arms and legs used to go numb regularly and especially during sleep. That issue is pretty much solved. For a long time, I would crave a cigarette right after a meal or when I had a beer. Now I find the smell of cigarettes disgusting. And I drink red wine instead of beer and have done so since age sixty. My favorites always seem to be wines that are expensive, with Caymus Cabernet leading the way.

Chapter 42

Wabasca Fishing

After I transferred from Calgary to Spruce Grove, Alberta (just west of Edmonton), with Atco Structures in 1979, I found that I was joining a team of employees that were a little on the wild side. Bob Boisvert was a fisherman working full-time at Atco. Wayne Johannson worked in the shop as superintendent when he wasn't fishing. When they found out that I had a winterized motor home, I became their new best friend. Bob would show up to work on a Friday morning with his boat, fishing equipment, Kielbasa (polish sausage), and beer, fully expecting that I would go home and get the motor home. The road to Lake Wabasca near Slave Lake in northern Alberta could more aptly be described as a trail in many places. Much of it was gravel and dirt through native Indian-owned land. The rule was that nothing you brought would be stolen if you left the motor home unlocked, except for alcohol. And if you locked up the motor home, it would be broken into by native Indians looking for booze.

There were two lakes at Wabasca. One was a deep lake, with gigantic lake trout, and the other was shallow, with perch and walleye. The latter also was home to some of the largest northern pike in the world. We called them jackfish. When you caught one, you avoided their sharp teeth by cutting the line and giving up on the hook.

The trick was to drop your hook to the bottom as quickly as you could and to jig off the bottom, where the desirable, great-tasting fish were swimming. On one trip, we neglected to bring anything other than Kielbasa and cheese to eat. Usually we could live off the land. The fishing was impossible, given poor weather conditions, so we pulled out our shotguns to go hunting. The only problem was that Bob had brought the wrong ammunition. He had brought slugs. It is hard to shoot ruffled grouse with slugs, considering that each slug was larger than the body of the grouse. However, the gunfire stunned the ruffled grouse enough that they would fall to the ground, where we could grab them. I think we survived the weekend on three grouse, which, combined, might be the equivalent of one-quarter of a chicken.

We used the leftover slugs on a lonely outhouse along the route. We decided that the leftover slugs would bring in enough fresh air to overcome the smell inside it. On another trip in early spring, we were on the lake when half of the ice was melted, leaving a good portion of open water and lots of very hungry lake trout. At one point, my lure was hanging over the edge of the boat, and a trout jumped out of the water and hit the lure so hard that it spun around my rod until the fishing line was tightened around the rod. The wind suddenly came up strong late in the afternoon, just as the sun was setting, and we found that our passage back to shore was blocked by ice blown to shore by the wind gusts. It was becoming very cold as we headed to a shoreline unknown to us and a long distance from our truck. Walking through the heavy woods in muskeg while carrying our boat on our heads was not fun. And we were banking on arriving at the gravel road at some point as it became dark. We were also relying on our direction being accurate, by watching for moss on the trees (always on the north side).

The muskeg was about twelve-eighteen inches deep at this point, so walking was often difficult. The bottom of the muskeg was frozen, so, at times, it was slippery, as well. Frankly, even with years of winter-camping experience, I was worried. Being lost is one thing. Being lost, wet, and cold is another. We had no cell phone (cell phones did not exist back then) and no flashlight. At least the three of us had a boat for shelter. Just as I was about to suggest we build a stopping place for the night, we came upon the road. We quickly dropped the boat and headed for the truck. I don't believe I have ever been so physically exhausted. And relieved. The freezing-cold retreat back to our warm motor home seemed almost like a welcome chore. We didn't let worry disrupt our productivity, as we charged through the forest as hard as we were able to so. Endurance builds character. And, boy, were we some kind of characters! In life, you should always check the score sheet and make sure that you aren't running for a finish line that doesn't exist. Our finish line was clear. Is yours? Do you have a finish line? Or are you floating aimlessly through life? Do you let things just happen to you? Or do you make things happen?

A lion has to run as fast as he can to catch a gazelle, or he will starve to death. A gazelle has to run as fast as he can, or the lion will kill him. Every day should find you going full speed at whatever you undertake and squeezing the juice out of life.

Chapter 43

Friends

Choose your friends carefully.

You will always be judged by the company you keep.

Over the years, I have enjoyed sharing my life with many who became close friends. My childhood friends include Cameron Moore, who taught me all about Mormons and the life that a Mormon family enjoyed. His family lived just a few houses down from me in Calgary, when I was about eleven years of age. I was a Baptist hanging out with a Mormon, but I don't remember anything (that mattered) that was that much different about us. His family didn't drink caffeine, but our street had numerous families of differing nationalities, so that didn't seem like much, given the diversity of my friends. When we did celebrate, it was not about our diversity; it was about our unity as Canadians. Remember that one.

My best friend through high school in Calgary was Danny Byrne. We played chess after school, and when his parents left him home while they visited their homeland in Ireland, we held a giant party for other fifteen-year-old friends in his basement and drank most of the homemade red wine that his parents had stocked. I have never been so sick in my life. I had arrived late to the party because I had to collect for my newspaper route. So, by the time I had arrived, I was way behind. Not knowing any better, I chugalugged an entire bottle to catch up. I awoke hours later on the thick white shag carpet in a pool of vomit and red wine. I was not able to drink wine again for about forty years. Danny was Catholic, so we attended different schools. His girlfriend was much older than he was, and his parents disapproved of their relationship until she presented them with a grandchild. Funny how that works. Years later, in 1987, Danny drove from Calgary to Houston to attend my wedding to Sherry.

BASS - Rob, Val, John, Kim, Jim, Sherry, Jim, and Robyn

Jim with United Methodist Men of Trietsch at the Marluc Bella Vita Ranch

Margo Williams was Judy's best friend, and it was she who introduced me to her friend, Judy Sundell. Judy and I married three years later. Margo stuttered a lot and always had issues with boyfriends and parents. I always enjoyed hanging out with her because our being together was never boring. She was at the railroad crossing and was the last person to see my brother in a car on the opposite side of the tracks as a day-liner hit the car trying to beat the train, killing my brother.

Dale Gates was much younger than I, but we shared many common interests when we met in Spruce Grove, Alberta, where I worked for Atco Structures. Dale was branch manager for Atco in Grande Prairie, Alberta. Our paths crossed many times over the years. He was my best man when Sherry and I married in Houston, and I was his best man at his wedding, as well. His father was president of Spartan Drilling, and, with Dale's reference, I became general manager of the Spartan Drilling Operations in Tioga, North Dakota. In later years, on my reference, Dale became branch sales manager at Space Master Buildings in Houston, Texas, where I was the commercial sales manager.

While working at Space Master in Houston, I became good friends with Dale Wheeler, who was a construction contractor for our company. I learned much about construction from Dale. He was a recovering alcoholic and drug addict, who died on a hospital stretcher and then came back to life. He recalled vivid memories of waking up in heaven and of being told he was being sent back to fulfill his purpose. From that day forward, he followed God's word and became a prison minister, helping many criminals to restore their lives and follow our Lord and Savior, Jesus Christ.

I attended one of Dale's sermons to the the jailed prisoners in Harris County Jail. It was frightening at times, but a very worthwhile and moving experience.

God has blessed me with many friends. Randy Guttery, Dave Meyer, and Dave Casey are my hockey buddies. We've made many trips all over Canada and the United States, following the Dallas Stars, the NCAA Frozen Four Championships, and Olympic hockey.

Sherry and I have attended the same Everyday Christians Sunday school class since 1990, and our classmates are our most cherished friends. You just don't spend that much time with people without coming to love them like family. In the same way, we have lived in the same home since 1999, and our cul-de-sac neighbors are also cherished friends.

Many of my business relationships have developed into strong friendships, and those friends include David Hammer and Jay and Bettye Rodgers. We were the founders of a nonprofit mentoring and training organization called Biz Owners Ed, which recently completed its fifth year in operation.

I have also made friends at my Rotary Club, where many of my Christian business friends gather weekly to support those in need. Steve Cox is the president this year, and it was he who helped me sell our commercial property and purchase our ranch property.

David Tedesco and I loved political discussions. He was a very talented musician and could play about any musical instrument. His knowledge of history was unending. We traveled through Italy together during the 2006 Winter Olympics. He enjoyed a glass of fine red wine with cheese and chocolate, just as I did. He became my financial advisor and taught me many important lessons about debt, investing, and finance. When I needed a long-term insurance policy in order to grow our business, he stated in clear terms that I had about two weeks to lose eight pounds. I did accomplish that task, knowing that the consequences meant that our business would not grow. You see, the bank would not lend us much-needed working capital without that insurance in place. David died last year after a brief struggle with a brain tumor—after he started exercising and lost weight and went back to school to get his MBA. The first sign of the presence of the brain cancer was his going to work and not remembering where his office was. I miss him.

Family reunion in Cochrane

5 generations with Mom, Judy, Dominyc, Grandma Attrell, and Jennifer

Granddaughters Delilah and Eloise

Jim and Granddaughter Chloe

Judy, Connor, Tim, Renee, and Ed at Connor's High School Graduation

Mom and children in Victoria

Family Reunion at the Richardson Farm

Uncle Clay, Aunt Connie, Aunt Cheryl, Uncle Bob, Aunt Isobel, and Uncle Ken

Devonne and Stephany with Samiah and Chase)

Jordan, Trisha, and Faith

Family at Trisha's wedding

Uncle Ken with children

Chapter 44

Politics

The United States has been on a long cultural downhill slide. Our culture and our policies as a nation have disregarded the value of human life, the sacredness of marriage, undermined parents in the raising of their children, banned God from the public square, removed prayer from school, and mocked every traditional value that in the past held our nation together. Our Founding Fathers were not perfect, but they acknowledged their imperfections and their deep reliance on God.

I voted for Pierre Trudeau and the Canadian Liberal Party soon after the government changed the legal voting age to eighteen years of age and announced that they would take from the rich and give to the poor. I was a young fellow with a growing family and was poor, so that was enough for me. Soon after that, I discovered that nothing was free. Trudeau was handing out goodies to get elected, and his strategy worked. I found myself unemployed and unable to pay my mortgage because of the social programs and excessive taxation and regulation brought in by Trudeau and the left-wing political party that he led. That experience taught me important lessons about responsibility. Freebies become entitlements. That which is given and not earned becomes an anchor on our society. It's one thing to help others and quite another to expect government to take on that role. We should lift up people and not tear down those that have become successful through their own efforts. You cannot lift up people unless you are on higher ground and have become successful at life. Liberals think that you lift up others by picking them up and bearing their entire weight to get them to the next level. No, you cannot be successful in that way, because those others that you help will expect you to continue to bear their weight. It is human nature. The correct way is to reach down, once you are at the higher level, and lend your hand to others, while they do the hard work of pulling themselves up and holding your arm of hope and help. Some people do not want higher ground, and that's okay. Much is expected of those that God blesses, and many would rather just stay where they are in life. You can bring a horse to water, but you can not make it drink.

After I became an American citizen in 1993, I ran for city council in Highland Village, Texas. I wanted to give back in some way to my new country. My opponent was accused of being a Peeping Tom at the televised candidates forum, so I developed a pretty good head start on him. In fact, I was fishing at Port Aransas on election day with my good friend Gene Hammond, a vendor to Space Master, where I worked. I won in a landslide.

At my first council meeting, residents complained that children were forced to walk on the roadway on their last block toward McAuliffe Elementary School. When I determined that the sidewalk construction cost was about $3,000.00, I stuck up my hand and made a motion that we spend the $3,000.00 and immediately undertake the necessary construction. The mayor and city manager both smiled and then enlightened me about the long, yet necessary, process that was first required. It took a year to build that sidewalk. After two years on the council and with my new baby son, Luke, on the way, I decided not to run again. Instead, I supported new candidates. There were four council members up for reelection, and they needed to be replaced. They had voted against selling advertising by our local merchants at our ballpark, which would have helped our sports programs for kids. The new candidates that I supported were Fred Busche, Bill Irwin, Jim Sloan, and Gary Kloepper. The initials of their last names were BISK, so I ordered numerous signs with simply "BISK" on them and placed them all over the streets of the community just weeks before the election. This became a big topic of conversation because no one, except me, knew what "BISK" stood for.

On the day before election day, I revealed what "BISK" meant, with new signs showing the candidates' names. I then erected and organized tents, staffed by supporters, at City Hall early on election day morning. It quickly became clear that our campaign made it easy for residents to remember who to vote for, and "BISK" won in a landslide that day. Over the next few years, I stayed very involved with city elections and supported candidates as their manager on occasion, and Sherry and I served as Parks Bond chairpersons one year.

When I worked for MPA Modular in Arlington, Texas, we were awarded the construction of a relocatable security building for temporary use at the entrance gates to the White House in Washington, D.C. Part of the requirement was to deliver and to set up the wheeled building, with its many special features, on a specific day and a specific time, when President Clinton was not at home. I became friends with the Secret Service supervisor, and he gave me a personal tour of the White House. He showed me the private room where Clinton and Monica Lewinsky (and others) had their private sexual adventures. When I asked him about respecting the president, he said that he was not required to respect the

Bisk Sign from City Election 2001

president. His only responsibility was to defend the president. He felt strongly that a married president having sex with an intern in the White House was entirely inappropriate and a criminal activity. I feel that way, as well. He also shared with me that the White House Secret Service personnel kept track of First Ladies and foul language. He felt (and told me so) that Hillary Clinton had set a new record for the most "F" words in the same sentence. The Secret Service supervisor also claimed that she did not like or appreciate Secret Service personnel and that she was the rudest First Lady in history.

In 2014, I volunteered to serve as a part of the security team at the State Republican Party Convention in Fort Worth. My job was essentially, along with many others, to make certain that only registered individuals entered the premises and that no one interfered illegally with the process. I found myself standing near and protecting some very powerful and influential political leaders. In 2016, I was appointed to the position of precinct chairperson in Highland Village and then was appointed to the State Republican Party Convention as a delegate for Texas state Senate, District 12. That was a unique experience. Can you imagine 3,500 average individuals like me (very few of us politicians) in one giant hall, praying together out loud and in unison for our country? That weekend was a moving experience, when I made many friends, and it solidified my conservative leanings extensively.

What I'll never understand is how liberal-leaning leaders think. Here are some examples. To liberal leaders, it's okay to abort the unborn but not to execute mass murderers? How can we raise our children to believe that life has value when our culture executes the unborn? To liberal leaders, the results of so-called climate change/global warming are more important than securing our borders? In the 1970's, at the peak of the industrial age and all its pollution, every scientist in the world was warning us that the evidence all pointed toward our world entering into an ice age. That science has disappeared. Why? To liberal leaders, when a drunk runs over someone in his car, it's the drunk person's fault, but when a terrorist or a mass murderer shoots someone, it is the gun or the NRA that is at fault?

AAA doesn't earn anything when you buy an automobile and they charge a fee to train and educate car owners. So when a drunk driver kills a child should we blame AAA? They are no different than the NRA in that regard. The Florida school shooting blame lies at the feet of the FBI, the cowardly armed policeman who was there and did nothing. It's time we hardened our schools like we do our airports and sports arenas. Our children are more important than those that enter airports or sports arenas so why are they not treated like we care more? And we should allow willing and trained educators to arm themselves. They all care about our children and are no less responsible than our armed police officers.

To liberal leaders, the government creates jobs, and not businesses? They need an education in economics apparently. To liberal leaders, conservatives hate women, minorities, and homosexuals. Conservatives don't divide up people by race, sex, and religion. They see people. Not color. The racists are often the ones doing the complaining.

You just know we are heading in the wrong direction when we find that our children are told in school that they may actually be a boy stuck in a girls body because they like playing with toy car but they can change their sex anytime that they want. Liberals want to fund Planned Parenthood where more than 90% of that so-called plan results in abortion and often the sale of baby body parts for research. Women should have the right to choose but that choice should end once they have made the decision to have sex. The unborn should have a vote in all future decisions from that point forward.

To liberal leaders, the government should provide all the safety nets for citizens (such as Social Security, Medicare, and Medicaid) and not the family? Certainly we need safety nets but not ones that can and are easily abused and designed to get votes and stay in power. To liberal leaders, the high-income earners have enough financial resources to support the rest of us, so they will vote to redistribute their earnings through excessive taxation? Problem is they want to tax high income earners and not the wealthy. Worse yet, these liberals are (or are led by) the wealthy liberal elite. They don't have to work.

President Trump just signed a new tax plan that eliminates tax breaks for the wealthy and these hypocrites are crossing the stages of America and using their media to complain. No more writing off $50,000.00 per month alimony payments. No more writing off $250,000.00 property taxes on mansions. No more writing off $150,000.00 in sales tax on a new yacht. No more writing off state income tax on the federal tax return. It's no wonder they are angry and spreading unbelievable propaganda. An example of such nonsense is the supposed war on women by conservatives? Every single elected position in Denton County where I live is held by republicans and it is one of the fastest growing counties in America. Our county judge is a woman. Our county commissioner is a (black) woman. Our mayor is a woman. Our state senator is a woman. They lead the charge, make the rules and do a great job of representing us.

To many liberal leaders, God is a myth and religion does not belong in government? How can liberal political leaders believe this propaganda, let alone spread it as if it were the truth? My experience is that liberals believe far too much that just is not true. Just as you can't see God, you can't see gravity, wind, radio waves, heat, cold, love, or heat. But you can feel them, and they do exist. The U.S. Constitution makes it clear that government should stay out of religion, but it also makes it clear that God should stay in government.

I have some ideas on how to change things for the better. For example, some of us are fortunate enough that we do not need Social Security and the reimbursement of the significant amounts of money that we contributed during our working years. So why not allow potential new Social Security recipients, at their option, to take a one-time cash advance, to place it in a trust fund, and have it designated as a donor-assisted education fund for their grandchildren?

Our elected officials should never go to Washington and should convene Congress over the Internet. That would mean extensive travel for the lobbyists and influence peddlers and congresspersons spending more time in their districts. Then, let's have a representative for every 30,000, people as the U.S. Constitution intended. Once elected, they would serve one four-year term, with elections every year to replace 25 percent of the House of Representatives. All U.S. citizens would be on the same health care insurance plan as the rest of us, and unionized government employees would become a thing of the past. No candidates would get elected to the U.S. Congress unless they have (at one time) owned their own businesses or have passed a basic test in economics. I would grant amnesty (not citizenship) to all illegal immigrants after our borders are secured—unless they are criminals (in which case I would deport them). Finally, citizenship should not be automatic if you were born in the United States to illegal alien parents.

President Obama put our country in economic danger with his policies. For eight years, we tolerated his excesses at golf, white-glove parties with his wealthy friends, traveling to fund-raisers for Democrats, vacationing with large entourages at taxpayer expense, and his clear disdain for conservatives and small business. I suspect that his thirst for political power has just begun. He is the master of deception. His propaganda is endless. Worst of all, he cares little for at least 50 percent of us. I only hope and pray that President Trump will be the leader that we truly need. Poverty is the worst since 1987, with 47 million Americans living in the poor house. 44 million Americans live on food stamps now.

For generations, 66–67 percent of Americans worked. Now only 63 percent can find work. For generations, our gross domestic product (GDP) grew an average of 3.2 percent annually. In the last few years, we've averaged just 2.1 percent growth. And worst of all, the U.S. government continues to spend far more than it brings in, and the national debt continues to grow past $19 trillion. Just to put that in perspective. You can fill a large briefcase with $100.00 bills, and that briefcase will hold $1 million. If you loaded a minivan with those briefcases, each filled with $1 million, you could fill that minivan with $1 billion. If you filled a football field with those minivans, each filled with $1 billion, you could fill that football field with $1 trillion. If you fill nineteen football fields with minivans, each filled with $1 billion in hundred-dollar bills, you would almost have enough cold, hard cash to equal our national debt, most of it run up in the last eight years of the Obama administration.

Think about this one. We were encouraged by President Obama not to judge Muslims by the actions of a few lunatics, yet he encouraged us to judge all gun owners by the actions of a few lunatics. You don't protect the innocent by taking guns away from the innocent. A gun is like a parachute. If you need one and don't have one, you'll probably never need one again. It's pretty basic common knowledge that he attempts to erase. And as I traveled, it was amazing to hear so many stories around the world of history where governments unarmed its masses and then selectively massacred the population. We U.S. citizens appear to be far from that happening, but so did past citizens of these other countries.

We are constantly warned that Social Security is soon going to run out of money, but these same politicians never warn us that the government is running out of money for ever-increasing welfare- and food-stamp programs. Social Security was created to be a safety net and it has become an entitlement. How many recipients don't need Social Security today because of their hard earned savings and resultant prosperity. How many recipients never bothered to try hard at life because they knew that they didn't have to?

The worst example of a country heading in the wrong direction is the United States paying its military poverty-level salaries and cutting benefits to its veterans, while providing benefits to illegal immigrants and providing gender-neutral facilities in border-holding cells for captured illegal immigrants. President Trump has taken corrective action early in his administration to empower our military to its former place with sufficient size and equipment to keep us safe.

In the presidential election of 2016 President Trump won 2,600 heartland counties and Hillary Clinton won 500 wealth-concentrated counties. That was a clear victory for the middle class who appear to be taking back America from the wealthy liberal elite who thought they could control the population through their media. Thanks to twitter our President was able to communicate truth directly to Americans absent liberal spin.

Chapter 45

My Parents

We often hear our children talk, and we realize we should have been more careful of what they heard us say. I still remember my dad, a happy person, singing, "I don't care if the sun don't shine; I get my loving in the evening time." I am certain that I was pretty young, because I also remember not understanding the words but experiencing his happiness and joy. Dad was always building something and volunteering somewhere. He was a scoutmaster of a Boy Scout troop and liked to make things himself.

Mom and Dad

I still have a leather bag that he made himself, including his stenciled initials. Our backyard on 7th Street in Calgary had a significant drop from the alley to the house. He built a concrete retaining wall about four feet tall and backfilled it from a pile of dirt that he had delivered. When I was five or six, I remember riding in the back seat of his National Supply Company car with a 7 7/8" drill bit, as he made an emergency delivery to a drilling rig. He instructed me on how to shoot a .22 caliber rifle on one of those field trips. A seagull flew by at a distance, so he demonstrated how I could use a shotgun in a similar manner if I were hunting ducks. He never expected to bring that seagull down with a twenty-two, but he did. He then explained that shooting seagulls was illegal. I remember how bad he felt. When I misbehaved, he gave me a choice of a spanking with his belt or time out in my bedroom.

I always chose the belt. It delivered short-lived pain. Dad helped me get my first car and my first real job. When Judy and I found out that she was pregnant (at age 18), he was the one whom I told. He asked me what I was going to do. I asked, "Get married?" He said, "That is correct." He informed my mom as she lay in bed. I can hear him today. "Doreen, you're going to be a Grandma." Within minutes, he had called our pastor and had the wedding scheduled for that same weekend at Kingsland Baptist Church. Jennifer was born six months later. Mom was always home when we were young. I came home from school for lunch at age thirteen, and Mom's eyes were wide, as she told me that President Kennedy had been shot in Dallas.

That confirmed my childhood fear of the United States, where all sorts of bad things were happening in the 1960s. Tornadoes, hurricanes, flooding, college campus shootings (for example, at Kent State University on May 4, 1970), massive car wrecks, antiwar protests, airplane crashes, drugs, threats of nuclear bombs, and an oncoming ice age. The United States seemed to me such a undesirable place to live in. I felt very safe at home in Calgary with my family. Mom was

Peter, Mom, Jim, Dad, and Trisha at Mom and Dad's 40th anniversary

Trisha, Peter, Jim, Mom, and Dad in Vancouver

Auntie Guite, Uncle Roy, and Mom

Dad with his brother, Uncle Ken

Charles and Jane Stewart with Marissa

always there for me—even with three younger children to care for. When the judged decided that I had come in second place in the school high-jump championship, she quickly challenged the judge. I was happy with a ribbon of any kind. When my brother, Kim, was killed in a car-train collision, she was devastated. It took a very long time for her to grieve. She was the youngest child of a very strict English couple.

When we visited Grandpa and Grandma Upton in Victoria, British Columbia for the first time, we were told that children were to be seen and not heard. Grandpa wore an apron as he carved the roast beef, and hardly a word was spoken as we ate. Mom started working when I was in high school, and she bought a used 1959 pink-and-white Ford station wagon. I had met Judy about that time and carved our initials in the dashboard. My mom was not impressed. I had much fun in that car. Mom let me take friends out to the drive-in theater. The car held about ten of us just fine. After one such event, my mother was driving me home, when an empty whiskey bottle rolled out from underneath her seat. I remember quickly saying, "Mom, did you take up drinking?" She gave me that look that only moms can give.

We all had dinnertime chores, including saying grace, which was usually something like, "God is great; God is good; let us thank him for our food." I disliked washing or drying the dishes, so I would trade chores with my younger brothers and sister. I preferred to set the table or clean off the table. Mom had a schedule posted on the kitchen wall, but she didn't seem to mind my trading chores with my siblings as long as the dinnertime chores were all taken care of. Mom left Houston a few years after Dad passed away (prostate cancer at age 66) and moved to Nanaimo, British Columbia, near my brother, Peter, and his family. She celebrated her ninetieth birthday at the time of this writing. I am not sure how she has lived so long, given that she has rarely concerned herself about eating healthy food or exercised. Dad, on the other hand, exercised regularly and tried to live a healthy lifestyle. I guess longevity has much to do with the gene pool. Mom swam in it, and Dad didn't. I do miss him.

Chapter 46

Marriage

Women have the last word in any argument. Anything a man says after that is the beginning of a new argument. A woman worries about the future until she gets a husband. A man never worries about the future until he marries. A woman marries a man, expecting he will change, but he doesn't. A man marries a woman, expecting that she won't change, but she does.

Jim and family at wedding to Judy

There is an old saying: "No one is perfect until you fall in love with them." I was sixteen, when I met Judy Sundell at high school. She and her friend, Margo Williams, hung out at the K Restaurant in the Kingsland Community near Henry Wise Wood High School in Calgary. Margo was very outgoing and a bit of a flirt. She realized quickly that I liked Judy after she had invited me to sit in the restaurant booth with them.

Judy lived in the apartments across the street. Gus, her dad, didn't like me at all. When I came over to pick up Judy, he would immediately go to his bedroom. Margaret, her mom, was very friendly. Except for a short period of time when we were upset with each other (she dated another guy for a while), Judy and I were together most of the time, except during school hours. We found ourselves in the Southwood library a couple of years later, trying to figure out how she got pregnant and what all that meant. By the time we were twenty-three years old, we had Jennifer, Chris, and Tim in our young family. Judy was a quiet introvert. She didn't learn to drive until age thirty or so and enjoyed relaxing with a book or watching television. I was working three jobs during those years and playing or coaching hockey the rest of the time. We really had little in common except for our children. When I found work with Spartan Drilling in Montana (after moving from North Dakota), Jennifer and Tim moved there with me, while Judy and Chris stayed in Stony Plain. We lost our home to foreclosure, and, instead of moving to Montana to join us, Judy moved in with a friend. She had a job at a hotel bar in Spruce Grove. It looked to me that she had decided to part ways. I bought her a new Volkswagen station wagon, hoping she would move to Montana and return to her family. Eventually, she did, only to find that I was being transferred to Houston. Shortly after moving to Houston, she started seeing a bartender where she worked, and we divorced. I was awarded custody, but, between poor parenting skills, a job with a struggling oil-patch employer, and depressed teenagers, life was not good. I did learn how to make a large variety of hamburger-helper meals.

It was about then (1984) that I met Sherry Stewart at Spoons, a restaurant on Gessner near Interstate 10 in Houston. I fell in love immediately. She was studying psychology full time at the University of Houston. She had been single since her early twenties and lived in a two-bedroom apartment just off Memorial near downtown Houston. With my kids and her studies, it was difficult to get much time together. I bought her an Apple IIe computer so that we could spend more time together. Her internship was fortunately at Baylor College of Medicine in Houston, so we started planning our marriage, which took place in a Methodist church on D-day in June 1987. Just

Sherry and Jim

Jim and Sherry in Galveston

as the service began, almost as if we were being cleansed of the past and renewed for the future, it rained hard outside the church. The noise of the rain on the roof ended as we were pronounced man and wife. Our honeymoon was spent in Bermuda. I had won a company-paid trip there, so we added on a few days. We found that our rented home had been ransacked while we were away. Sherry lost all of her jewelry, including class rings. We then bought a very nice home in Inverness Forest, north of Houston, where I worked. That home was flooded twice, so I was able to get a transfer to the Space Master Dallas branch just after Marissa was born in October 1989. Our new home in Highland Village, Texas, was a perfect community in which to raise children, and Luke was born in March 1993. Sherry and I attended Trietsch Memorial United Methodist Church in Flower Mound, Texas, upon our arrival and have been in the same Sunday school class since 1990 (www.tmumc.org). We have made many friends, and I could not imagine living anywhere else but here. We moved about half a mile (in 1999) after waiting for about a year to find the perfect home in the same community among our friends. We bought our two-story home on Remington Terrace the same day that it was listed for sale. We have since built a pool and added on a bedroom and a game room upstairs. It's on the end of a cul-de-sac and backs up to a green belt. God is good, but we had to patiently wait for him to open that door.

> "I never know what to get my father for his birthday. I gave him a hundred dollars and said, 'Buy yourself something that will make your life easier.' So he went out and bought a present for my mother."
>
> —Rita Rudner

Chapter 47

Children

"Having a child fall asleep in your arms is one of the most peaceful feelings in the world."

A woman knows all about her children. She knows about dentist appointments, romances, best friends, favorite foods, secret fears, and hopes and dreams. A man is vaguely aware of some short people living in the house.

It was an impactful moment in my life when the nurse put Jennifer in my arms in the hospital delivery room in March 1970. She weighed about seven and a half pounds. She quickly became a family favorite, because she was the very first grandchild and great-grandchild

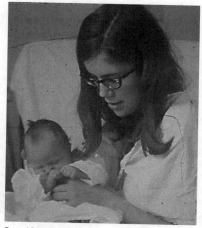

Jennifer and Judy

in our family. My sister worked and worked until Jennifer took her first step. She loved to push Dad's wheeled orange footrest around the living room, and her giggle was contagious. Christopher came along about twenty months later. He weighed about eight and a half pounds. We got him a puppy for one birthday, and when we asked him what he wanted to name it, he said "Bowser." He finally agreed on "Goldie." Timothy was born about twenty-six months later and weighed about nine and a half pounds. Judy decided that it was time to stop right there and had her tubes tied immediately. Tim was outgoing and fearless. When he was a toddler, other children with any kind of food would avoid him, because he would help himself to half their cookie

Jennifer with Cephas and children

Chris, Judy, Jennifer, and Tim

Chris and Kelly

Chloe, Tim, and Connor

Jennifer and Cephas in Nova Scotia

Luke, Sherry, and Marissa with Toby and Copper

or ice cream (trying to be polite of course). All three of our children played hockey and enjoyed our camping trips. Looking back, Judy and I did move very often, which made it difficult for our children to form long-term friendships. I have some regret about that issue. Jennifer and her husband, Cephas, now have five children and one grandchild. Kerry was born in June 1988, Dominyc in July 1990, Devonne in August 1992, Devereaux in August 1993, and Michaela in April 1997. Samiah was born in 2017 to Devonne and Stephany. She is my first great-grandchild.

Tim and Renee have two children; Connor was born in October 1995, and Chloe was born in July 2001. Sherry and I had Marissa in October 1989 and Lucas in 1993. Marissa weighed about seven pounds, and Lucas weighed close to eight pounds. They played together constantly as young children. Marissa did most of the talking.

Jim, Luke, Sherry, Marissa, and Josh in Scotland

Jennifer, Renee, Tim, and Cephas at Mom's 90th Birthday in Nanaimo

Both were excellent students and had a passion for learning new things. Marissa has completed her doctoral training and psychology internship and is working part-time while caring for (along with husband Josh) her daughters, Delilah (born May 2014) and Eloise (born May 2016). She is expecting another daughter (Cecilia) in April 2018. Luke graduated from the University of Texas at Dallas with a degree in Mechanical Engineering and is employed by a small engineering firm in Irving, Texas. Both Luke and Marissa have lived in the same community and have attended the same schools for their entire lives. I think that has proven to be a good thing.

D-day took place on June 6, 1944. The lead airplane on the flight from England was filled with the most modern radar and radio technology of the time, along with the American commander. Seventy years later, that airplane was discovered in the weeds of an airplane wrecker yard in Wisconsin. The workers there pulled it out of the field and were amazed that it actually started. The past was lost, but, now, it is found. In many ways, I feel like that airplane. I was so busy working and earning a living as a young man that I forgot to "squeeze the juice" out of my relationship with my children. One day, they were toddlers, and, the next day, they were borrowing the keys to the car. Children growing up happens quickly. And being in a different country didn't help, especially when grandchildren came along. I now have nine grandchildren and one great-grandchild. It is hard to believe. They are all little miracles, and I expect much of them. And I will be there for them when they ask for help. Again, it is a long-distance relationship in most cases, but I am making the best of that situation when I am able to do so. Spending time with Delilah and then Eloise, as well, has been very special. We have crackers and cheese when I come home in the afternoon and then watch their favorite kids' movies over and over again. Delilah has learned the song, "God Is Bigger Than the Boogie Man," and I never tire of her singing that Veggie Tale inspiration. Teaching these baby girls new things is fascinating. The smallest things are all new to them. The joy of watching them succeed and accomplish helps to fill that void of my life as a young and often-absent father.

Marissa, Cecilia, Delilah, Josh, and Eloise

Chapter 48

Siblings

Mom and Dad had four children. I was born first, in Edmonton, Alberta, in December 1950. Kimberly (Kim) was born in Calgary, in November 1952. Peter was born in Calgary, in June 1955, and Patricia ("Tricia") was born in Calgary, on April Fool's Day 1957. Like most families of the day, we were closely knit and spent most of our time together, playing board games, listening to the radio, or playing outside. We all had chores. Tricia seemed always to get preferential treatment as the only girl. We guys had to share the same bath, while she got her own hot water all to herself. On Saturday nights, Dad would take one of Mom's old nylon stockings

Jim, Trisha, Peter, and Kim

Mom and Trisha

and place it on our heads to keep our hair flat to our heads for church on Sunday mornings. Of course, Tricia didn't have to undergo that embarrassment. Kim died at age fifteen in a car-train wreck. When she was young, Tricia married Dean and divorced him after a short period of time. She then married Kim Kindopp and had two children. Ashley was born in April 1983, and Jason was born in August 1984. They divorced, and Tricia then moved to Penticton, British Columbia, where she raised her kids. All three returned to Calgary years later, where they live now. Peter joined the RCMP and moved to Vancouver

Jim, Peter, Kim, Trisha, and Dad in Victoria

Island, working in different marine cities over the years. He married Christine Lucas and had two sons, Brian born in February 1981 and Kevin born in March 1983. Peter and Christine divorced, and Peter married Heather, and they had two sons together. Daniel was born in February 1999, and Steven was born in April 2000. They live in

Sonya and Keith Renner

Nanaimo, British Columbia. We get together as often as possible and enjoy our reunions—not only with them but also with our mother, who also lives in Nanaimo.

Chapter 49

Famous People

Over the years, I have met a few famous people. Of course, they include lots of hockey players, like Wayne Gretzky, Guy Carbonneau, and Bob Gainey. I had the pleasure of sitting beside Bob Gainey on a plane on the way to Calgary and beside Pudge Rodriguez, our famous Texas Ranger catcher on another plane ride. He was the nicest person. I met Troy Aikman at the airport during his rookie season. I met Nolan Ryan at a Republican fund-raiser in Houston, and he signed a baseball for me. I met Newt Gingrich, Mike Huckabee, and Ted Cruz at various political events.

I found Newt to be arrogant, Mike to be down-to-earth open and friendly, and Ted to be very guarded in everything he said. Nolan Ryan was definitely a favorite. He autographed a baseball for me and introduced me to the Harris County judge. My flight to Dallas while sitting in first class beside Pudge Rodriquez was one of the most entertaining two hours of my life. He was open about every question I asked and struck me as one of the most grounded sports personalities I could have the pleasure to know. Troy was very pleasant, as well, and put down his baggage to autograph my business card.

Chapter 50

Jobs and Careers

My first job as a paperboy was my first experience of a payday. Of course, I had to collect from my customers and be responsible for every paper delivered to me. Responsibility is not easily learned unless you experience the consequences of not being responsible. At age sixteen, I started working at the local Texaco station in Southwood in Calgary, pumping gas, cleaning windows, checking and changing oil, and repairing and replacing tires. The pay was $1.25 per hour. The part of the job I disliked was cleaning the restrooms and mopping all the floors at closing. After being fired for making an emergency battery-booster trip with the wrecker while I was intoxicated, I went to work across the corner at Southland and Elbow Drive for Irv, the owner of the Royalite Gas Station. The pay was the same, but I got to work with young friends rather than old guys. We bordered the local Sarcee Indian Reserve, where alcohol was a serious problem. Often we were asked to take (as payment) spare tires or car radios for a very small amount to pay for gasoline. It was not unusual for an Indian customer to put twenty-seven cents worth of gasoline in his tank because that was all the customer had. Once I bought an old Buick for about $50.00 and sold it the next day for not much more than I had paid for it. I smoked heavily and drank large quantities of Pepsi. It was no wonder that I had trouble gaining weight. The province had mandated that all motor vehicles must have their headlights' direction checked and adjusted, as needed. Irv became a licensed service provider and bought the machine and equipment. I would find large numbers of vehicles lined up for headlight inspection and adjustment when I opened the station on a Saturday morning. Today, it seems comical that no one wore seat belts back then and that one of the most dangerous features of our cars was the protruding radio knobs. In a collision, children would crash into the dashboard, and their heads would be severely punctured by the radio knobs. Rather than making seat belts a requirement, the government required the elimination of the radio knobs? Strange.

From gasoline jockey-hood, I became a trainee at the Bank of Nova Scotia on 7th Avenue and 6th Street SW in Calgary in 1969. During my first six months, I served as a bank teller. There were no calculators back then. I calculated the interest to be paid by using an old adding machine, on which I punched in the account balance for a day and then pulled the handle to enter that amount and print it on the tape. That process was repeated for each day of the month. The numbers on the tape were then totaled, and the tape was removed from the adding machine and paper-clipped to the account card. I would then write on the tape with a pen the number of days in the month, divide it by hand into the total of the daily balance on the tape to arrive at an average daily balance. I would then multiply that amount by 365 days and multiply that by the current annual interest rate, whatever that rate was, to come up with the interest due for a year. Then I would divide that amount by twelve months to come up with the interest to be paid for the month. All this was done by hand, every month, and then double-checked by the bank accountant. One day, I was over by $10.00 when balancing my teller box at the end of the day. I spent hours trying to figure out and reconcile the difference, but I couldn't. It was several weeks later that a deposit slip for $10.00 fell from the bottom of my teller box, where it evidently had been stuck. I found the work in the bank extremely boring—except for the monthly test of the bank branch gun. We would meet on a Saturday morning, open up the bank vault, pile up some old IBM cards in boxes, and fire the gun inside the vault into the boxes. The funny thing was that we were not allowed to carry the bank gun, even when transporting large amounts of cash to another bank. The branch manager held weekly poker games in the break room after hours, and occasionally he would invite me, on the condition that I lose the $50.00 (that he gave to me) to our bank customers. During the horse racing season, he would give me $800.00 in cash and a telex tape with the names of horses racing that day that I was to bet on. That telex came in from a bank in Saskatchewan. I was instructed to bet $50.00 to win, and $50.00 to place on each race and on a single horse. I got a flat tire on the way to the racetrack on one occasion and missed the first race. Heart pumping, I was relieved to find that the horse I was supposed to bet on was neither a win nor a place. Considering the excellent past win record of the telex tapes, I decided to bet the newly acquired $100.00 along with the rest on the next race. The horse turned out to be a large and powerful-looking gray mare. I watched in horror as she rounded into the stretch, tripped, and fell to the track, writhing in pain from a broken ankle. Some racetrack workers put her into a van on the track and closed the door. The next sound I heard was gunfire. That was my last race track experience.

Uncle Roy, my mom's brother helped me to get a new, more interesting job at Corbett's Wholesale, an automotive parts organization. I was assistant to the manager, which meant that I did everything that he didn't like to do, like ordering coffee supplies for the kitchen and balancing the company checking account monthly. It was a great experience, but there wasn't any room upward in the organization. I especially did not enjoy auditing the four pricing employees. My job was to look for errors and inform my supervisor. I was the "snitch," and that didn't suit me.

My father helped me find my job, where he worked at Atco Structures. Tom Malloy was my direct supervisor, but Dave Olason, the contracts department manager, hired me. He wrote on the back of his business card my starting salary of $350.00 per month. With a mortgage payment of $94.00 per month, that seemed like a great salary. That was 1970, and inflation was running wild. What I could afford then I could not afford a year later. I was forced to transfer departments within the company in order to get the salary increase that I needed to support my growing family. Even with the raise, I had to work part-time at a gasoline station. The president of Atco Structures was twenty-seven years old and seemed old to me. Opportunities were endless; not only for me but also for the company. Our profit margins were gigantic. We manufactured all types of relocatable buildings at the old Canadian Air Force base on Crowchild Trail—from travel trailers, mobile homes, and office trailers to remote living quarters for 5,000 men and Hercules transportable camps for use in the Arctic. It was an exciting business. I learned all aspects of the business as project administrator with liaison to every department of the company. For a couple of years, I was the lease fleet administrator, with responsibility for billing, collections, repair, maintenance, transportation and the setup of thousands of relocatable buildings on lease to thousands of (mostly) oilfield, pipeline, timber, mining, and other industrial customers across western Canada. I was promoted to sales in 1977 and immediately discovered that I was an excellent marketing-and-sales representative because I knew the product and service more thoroughly than most of our staff, plus I enjoyed learning to match our products to our customers' needs. The oilfield-drilling business had really grown, and the company started a new specialty-sales organization, of which I was one of the first employees. I was able to transfer to the Edmonton area (near my hockey team: Wayne Gretzky and the Edmonton Oilers, of course), and I worked in the Spruce Grove office for about a year.

Brent Elton and Guy Turcotte (who has since become one of the wealthiest individuals in the world) coaxed me to leave Atco and be part of a new start-up oilfield-catering company called A-1 Camp Service. I quickly grew our business to maximum capacity, serving over thirty remote oilfield camps in Alberta that winter. Then the governing Canadian Liberal Party nationalized the oil industry, and all of our customers left town (or at least quit exploration). We opened up in Bryan, Texas, to serve an oilfield in the United States that was very active, with a concentration in the Giddings Field near Bryan, Texas. Our main customers were Spartan Drilling and Omni Drilling, both Canadian companies.

It was about then that Alan Gates (president of Spartan Drilling and my best friend Dale's father) called me to his office in Nisku, Alberta. I was hoping for more business because things were not good in the Canadian oilfields. What he asked of me was to move to North Dakota, along with rig eleven, and become his Williston Basin contracts manager. It was not what I expected, but the pay was pretty good. It seemed much better than unemployment, and I kinda liked adventure.

After a few months, Omni Drilling was shut down by their lenders, and Spartan Drilling took over the operation on a contract basis. That helped our overhead cost immensely. I ended up with two more drilling rigs, seven work-over rigs, and a transfer from the thriving metropolis of Tioga, North Dakota, to Sidney, Montana. The company promoted me to general manager of the operation. The state tree of North Dakota is a telephone pole, so Sidney was a visual improvement. Tioga had two restaurants—one open for breakfast and lunch and another open for supper. The same waitresses worked at both establishments. Of course, there were at least five bars. I became close friends with Gene Trudell in Sidney. He became my drilling superintendent. I went back to visit him and his wife, Nancy, recently. He hasn't changed a bit. Just older. Alan asked me to open a new Houston office close to Shell Oil, our best customer, so that I could develop additional customers for the Texas and North Dakota operations, and he promoted me to vice president of Sales and Marketing. I was able to foster the Shell relationship and to develop Exxon as a new customer, but the oilfield took a terrible turn for the worse. We could no longer sell our services to break even, much less to earn a profit. Our contract relationship with the Omni lenders was dissolved, and a major oil operator went bankrupt after we drilled a dry well for it, leaving us unable to continue business operations in the United States.

Alan asked me to return to Calgary as contracts manager for the company, but I had met Sherry and decided to stay in Houston. Alan and Dale started a new business enterprise called Enersave that had marketing rights to a patented flue-pipe product. I became the U.S. employee, and Dale, the Canadian employee. After about a year, it became apparent that the recession would bring an end to our financial resources, and, once again, I decided to stay in Houston.

I obtained my Texas real estate license and tried working both new homes and home for resale, but the market was just too tough. I finally found the perfect job for me through the grace of God in the help-wanted section of the newspaper.

Doug Alexander, the senior vice president of Space Master Buildings, flew into Houston from Atlanta and hired me on the spot. I showed up at the North Houston branch for work the following Monday. I introduced myself to the receptionist, who informed me that no one had told her of my hiring and that there was no furniture in my office. A few months later, the plan became apparent, as Doug fired the other salesperson and I became the branch manager. Once again, I found an excitement about my career with endless business and personal opportunities. I was on a small base salary, but the commissions from sales and leases were excellent. Sherry and I attended the annual Space Master Club event for top performers almost every year, with trips to such places as Bermuda, Acapulco, Puerto Rico, and Florida.

I grew the branch quickly by hiring great new employees, and I supervised all activities of the construction of a new model office. My friend Dale became branch manager when I was promoted to commercial sales manager over major projects. Then disaster struck. After two flooding episodes of our home, Sherry and I packed up and moved to Dallas. Ray Wooldridge, the president of Space Master, transferred me to the office north of Dallas in Carrollton, Texas, where I became branch manager. That happened in December 1989, just after Marissa was born. It was a fairly new branch, with much work required. After a couple of successful years, I was promoted to vice president and general manager of the southwest region of the company, with branches in Houston, Denver, Dallas, Fort Worth, and Denver. I made many friends in the industry, but I became very close friends with Gene Hammond at Indicom Buildings, one of my top suppliers. Gene and I loved to travel to Corpus Christi and go fishing. He was with me when I caught the trophy trout that sits on the wall of the den at our ranch lodge. I also became close friends with Doug Alexander at Space Master. When he was pushed aside and replaced by

Bob Coker, I just could not make the adjustment to new management, and I resigned from the company. Doug recently passed away during minor surgery, which caught me and other friends by surprise.

John Transue had left Space Master in Denver and started Advanced Modular Space. He and I started discussion, resulting in my resignation from Space Master and employment on a contract sales basis with John's new company. Business was good, but John took one half of the profits and contributed little, so I started Modular Space Corporation.

Modular Space Corporation was an inactive company, but I was able to obtain the rights to the name. Jerry Brown and I became partners, along with a silent partner (no ownership) named Mike Mount, the president of Indicom Buildings and a major supplier. In return for sharing the cost of accounting and receiving a monthly check to help with our overhead costs, we committed ourselves to purchasing our products from Indicom Buildings. We worked hard, but the timing was poor, and business was not good. I turned over full ownership to Jerry and helped with the overhead costs by leaving the company.

MPA Modular was an Arlington, Texas-based manufacturer of modular buildings. It wanted to start a leasing operation and hired me for $96,000.00 per year, with part ownership in the lease operation. It was a ninety-minute roundtrip drive for me from Highland Village to Arlington, but I enjoyed the challenge of the position. Having control over the manufacturing aspect of the business made for a much simpler process, with no middleman, very much like my ten-year Atco employment in Canada. The rental fleet grew quickly. I inquired about my formal ownership documents at my annual review and was told that I would have them within ninety days. Well, ninety days went by, and I was informed that another 30 days were needed. When I heard that the owner had secretly put the company up for sale (I had lots of friends in the business), I gave him a week to provide the contract documents. As it turned out, I doubt that he had ever fully intended to live up to his commitment. When I left, he asked me to stay on for another week. The buyer that he was working with didn't want the leasing operation, because the buyer's company was a supplier to mobile-office leasing companies and would be perceived as a competitor, putting their relationship at risk. Looking back, I should have just left. Somehow I felt sorry for him. And, of course, I had friends there that I didn't want to hurt. Jeff McLain was one of those friends. He would later become my vice president of Construction at Nortex.

Ray Wooldridge at Space Master was thrilled to hear from me and hired me back immediately. He was also (quietly) in the process of selling the business, and I would add much value to the sale. He said it would take several months and the buyer would likely want to transfer me to California. I had no intention of being transferred there, but I needed a paycheck. During the next few months of 1998, I silently put everything in place so that Nortex Modular Space could be in business immediately. During my last few weeks at Space Master, I landed a million-dollar (plus) contract with Conoco, but the paperwork process was lengthy. Ray called and asked me to call him and confirm receipt of the hard copy of the purchase order immediately upon receipt. Little did I know that our major competitor on that project was the Space Master buyer, none other than Williams Scotsman. Ray wanted the sale of that project to appear on his side of the ledger at closing. That made perfect sense to me. Of course, the first thing that Williams Scotsman did was to inform Conoco that he had bought Space Master and that the purchase order needed to be canceled and reissued to Williams Scotsman. When the Conoco buyer called me, I explained that I would still act as project manager and that I would make certain that the company received what it had expected. I let the "big boys" in the corporate offices fight out the purchase-order issue. Then, when I informed Williams Scotsman that I would not be moving to California, Williams Scotsman said that my employment would be terminated, with seven days pay. How nice of that company! I called my customer at Conoco, and, after explaining the new circumstances (he really disliked Williams Scotsman), he asked if I would consider coming to work for Conoco during the project construction as their representative, ensuring that Williams Scotsman performed up to expectations. Naturally, I agreed. I would finally get my opportunity to make life miserable for a much-despised competitor. When my Conoco buyer informed Williams Scotsman that I would be representing Conoco, Williams Scotsman reconsidered its position and its area manager called me to tell me so. He offered to put me on a base salary during the expected project time period that would equal my expected commission. I explained that I had started a business called Nortex Modular Space and that my new company could be hired to manage the project at $2,000.00 per week, plus all expenses paid, and that, during the contract period, Nortex would be competing with Williams Scotsman for business elsewhere. Now Williams Scotsman didn't like that, but it became backed into a corner as a result of its greedy foolishness. So, as a result, my first sale at Nortex was to my largest competitor. Best of all, my second sale just weeks afterward was one to a trucking company that terminated the lease on a Williams Scotsman office trailer and bought a much larger permanent modular office building from Nortex Modular Space. That transaction feels as good now, as I'm writing this, as it did then, when it happened. It was all good for the next twelve years that we owned the business. We grew rapidly and hired the best individuals that we could. We served a niche market with a high-quality, energy-efficient modular office and classroom building. We leased our product in-house. We built a model factory, where we developed building products that were more often than not manufactured in our partner vendor factories. At peak, we had 100 employees. Branches were located in Denver, Lewisville (Dallas), Houston, and Austin. Our leasing operation consisted of 1,000 buildings, generating $500,000.00 lease revenue per month. Most of our growth occurred during the severe economic downturn of 2008. The U.S. government (including the U.S. military) did not have the financial resources to erect new facilities, but it could lease our products under our GSA contract, and our products met the need for energy efficiency under that same contract. Churches were in that same boat. No competitor offered from inventory the quality that we offered. Professional subcontractors were attracted to us because of our reliability and financial stability. We always paid our bills on time and paid early if a discount was available. At some point, when the economy started to recover early in 2009, I saw my sixtieth birthday fast approaching, with no continuation plan in place. What exactly would happen if I died? Who would take over? Would the bank demand immediate repayment of the debt that we carried? Our children had no interest, much less the knowledge that was needed. My mentor during that time was Jerrell Jenkins of United Community Bank in Highland Village, Texas. Jerrell suggested that I contact David Hammer, who was a director of the bank. Within two years, David sold our business to Black Diamond Group of Calgary, Canada. The transaction was a unique reverse triangular merger, whereby our proceeds consisted mostly of Black Diamond publicly traded stock. There were no taxes on that transaction, but the cost basis in the stock was zero, making the sale of any Black Diamond stock that I had held taxable at full tax rates. Although the dividends on the stock were excellent (and paid monthly) and the business was growing, I did not want all of our eggs in one basket. During the next two years, I sold the stock and paid the taxes as the stock rose from $15.00 (Canadian dollars) to $30.00, split two for one down to $15.00, and rose to $35.00. Then the oilfield downturn struck. The stock is trading today at $2.00. My friend, Jay Rodgers, always said that the best time to sell was the time when it was too early to sell. He was right—not only about selling our business (which today is pretty much nonexistent, with less than ten employees) but also about selling the stock. It makes me sad to see what has happened to small businesses during the last few years under liberal government leadership, but it didn't help that the new owners at Black Diamond attempted to convert Nortex to an oilfield supplier at a time when the oilfield was "folding up" and going home. There is an old saying that when the past calls, don't answer it, because it has nothing new to offer. But, in my case, when the past calls, it will likely be a call from a friend or a past employee, and I very much enjoy those calls. So I always answer because, in spite of the outcome, that past was good. What I have learned is that everything decays with time. All great civilizations will disappear. It's the relationships that matter. The rest is just stuff that you can't take with you, anyway.

Within days of announcing my retirement from Nortex, I met with Pastor John Allen at our church. John wasn't aware that I had planned my retirement, when he asked me if I knew of anyone that might take the position of director of operations at our church and complete the construction of the new Family Life Center. Our associate minister had been appointed to his own church, leaving a void in the area of facility operations. Of course, this was a "God thing," and I found myself volunteering for the position. Six months (my first commitment) stretched into eighteen months, but I have to say that I very much enjoyed my employment during that time. John wanted me to pick an office, but I preferred not to have an office. Calls were automatically routed to my cell phone, even when I was in Australia. There were many challenges. It is said that if you look behind the curtains in a church, things do not usually look so holy. I can tell you from personal experience that people working at a church are no different from all people in terms of human failure. The main difference is a much higher level of caring about others.

After we sold Nortex, we formed Marluc, LLC, a corporation created to hold revenue-producing real estate. The timing was excellent because people were moving from all over America, where hard economic times were prevalent, to north Texas, where conservative values meant prosperity for business and therefore lots of new jobs. We acquired twenty-five residential properties and some commercial property over two years, and the homes were rented to quality tenants. We sold the commercial property when we determined that residential property made more financial sense. Best if all, we were deliberate about acquiring starter rental homes within a mile of our office, which is a two-bedroom patio home about a mile and a half from home. Dan Sarine was our accounting manager at Nortex and has worked as our property manager at Marluc for four years. Marluc has also recently acquired 188 acres, with a Barndominium (a metal building with a garage and a two-bedroom apartment) near Possum Kingdom toward Jacksboro, Texas. The construction of a new retreat for family, extended family, and nonprofits was completed in July 2017. The property has a wildlife exemption and three stock ponds and a new four-acre lake stocked with wide mouth bass and other supportive fish species. The lake is forty-one feet deep. It is my hope that Lake Godstone will be the place to go for wide mouth bass and for that to happen within the next five years.

Chapter 51

The Joy of Pets

People will give you love and grief and anxiety, but a pet will most often give you only joy. It won't talk back to you, and it will give you unconditional love and acceptance. Pets make great travelers, if you've got the right one and it's well trained.

What would life be without pets? My first pet was a grey Persian cat named Betsy. She would follow me to school sometimes, running under the cover of neighbors' hedges and trees, and she would often be waiting for me outside the school when the bell rang to end the day. She disappeared one evening, and, after walking all over the neighborhood, I found her in the basement of a new home under construction. Her fur on her back was hanging by a thread from some unknown cause, but she did heal up fine. Cats, like some humans, are natural-born adventurers and make excellent companions.

We would often take Betsy camping with us, and, on one occasion, we made the mistake of trying to hold her while we took down our tent and packed up to leave. Shaken by the noise, she took off, leaving my parents uncertain of what to do. Of course, I was certain of what to do and said I was staying until she returned to our campsite. Dad reluctantly unpacked everything, and, after setting up the camp, he left us with Mom, while he drove home to attend work the next day. Betsy did thankfully return late that evening to our campfire, and she lived to be almost twenty years of age. The waiting was worth it.

When my son Chris was about seven, we bought him a Lab cross for his birthday, and he named her Goldie. She quickly became one of the family. Always wagging her tail, she was best friends with each of us. She moved with us from Spruce Grove, then to Montana, and finally to Houston. Somehow she escaped from our yard when she was older and in poor health. We had just moved into a temporary home (townhouse) after our home flooded, and she may have been trying to return to the home she knew. We'll never know.

Betsy

We picked Mandy from a crop of Lab cross pups at a dog-rescue event. When we got her home, she ran to the corner of the backyard and cowered in the corner. She had endured abuse previously by a male owner, and it took years for her to feel comfortable coming to me when I called. She was especially good with Marissa and Luke and was their constant companion. She was also very good friends with our tabby cat Zerbert. When we moved from Creekside to Remington in Highland Village, a distance of less than a mile, Zerbert disappeared for some time, but we found that she had been adopted by a neighbor after she just showed up in her yard. Apparently, the food was better. Mandy lived to be about twelve, before losing the use of her legs. Putting her down was very difficult.

Sherry had lost her toy poodle, Bijou, to old age about the time we got Mandy, so I brought her a cute little poodle that we named Penny. Penny wasn't an especially great pet, but the kids adored her, until she drowned in our pool in a tragic accident. Most people wouldn't think of a pool as a danger to a dog, but that particular pool wasn't very friendly because we also lost Ashley, a dachshund cross in that same manner. We had adopted her after Sherry's parents passed, and Ashley had several age-related health problems.

Toby (Beagle) and Bogy (large male cat) came into our lives about that time, and they are now well-behaved senior citizens. Toby has issues, so we keep him penned up whenever we have guests. Pets can be finicky, moody, playful, and sad. The joy of a dog or a cat can add so much value to life.

Chapter 52

Marluc Bella Vita Ranch

Early in 2016, I started looking for ranch property within a couple hours drive of our home in Highland Village, Texas. My son-in-law, Josh Benners, enjoyed hunting, and, over a few months, we visited several properties, with a goal of finding a place that had an existing living quarters of some kind and a place where our family (including extended family) could spend time together.

We also wanted a ranch property that would be owned as an investment by Marluc, LLC and kept for the long-term.

I asked Steve Cox, a friend and a commercial real estate broker, to assist with the effort. Along the way, Lisa Healy and Charlotte Wilcox, also our friends and residential real estate agents, found a gem of a property within an hour's drive. It had a beautiful modern home and a lake, but the property was small and not a good hunting place. Charlotte was also our city mayor and it was Lisa that adopted our cat when she disappeared.

In April of 2016, Steve discovered a new 188-acre property with a Barndominium (a metal building with a two-bedroom apartment, a two car garage, and covered parking) that was recently listed and was located between Jacksboro and Possum Kingdom 100 miles away from our home.

The property had everything desired and more. Steve informed me that the new listing had two more viewing appointments the next day, so we made a full-price cash offer. The owners accepted and included their (almost new) tractor, complete with implements, as well as the apartment furniture.

I was very impressed with the construction of the Barndominium. It was simple but durable. After meeting the contractor (Duane Norvill, the owner of Norvill Construction of Jacksboro, Texas),

Ranch Lodge

Lake Godstone

I entered into a cost-plus contract for a new two-story lodge
(www.norvillconstruction.com). We were going to be building the lodge
on a pad cut into the limestone rock wall on the south of the property,
and we were also going to make a new two-acre fishing pond to be
located off the north side of the porch of the new lodge, where a dense
forest currently occupied the valley. That was the plan.

That valley had a creek running through it, with water runoff from
the 800 acres adjacent to the property on the south and west sides.
During heavy rain, that creek became a river.

In May 2016 Duane and I worked our way down the limestone
rock hill through the thick forest and poison ivy (during a heavy rain)
and down to the river. We carefully placed a painted steel stake five feet
above the river as our desired building pad location of the new lodge.

In August 2016, Wade Lake brought a bulldozer and an excavator
to the property and began the search for that stake and the preparation
of the building pad.

During the next seven–eight months, Wade, along with his sons
and other family members, would convince me to significantly enlarge
the size and depth of the pond and turn it into a lake forty-one feet
deep. We found that the limestone bed was fairly shallow and that a
bed of pure clay, perfect for dam construction, lay just beneath it. And,
better yet, just below that clay bed, lay a bed of blue-shale clay, the
perfect dam-topping material and perfect lake-bottom material.

Wade helped me in my desire to build the best bass-fishing lake
that we could. His many years of experience and expertise led to a
super-structure dam and a spillway with shallow pea-gravel ledges for
raising fish and a shoreline that was mostly up into the trees, creating
good cover for our fish.

I consulted with many experts about building a great bass lake
and selected an Arkansas supplier recommended by my friend,
David, of H Brands in Jacksboro, Texas. Bill at Fish Wagon helped to
determine the recommended mix, size, and quantities of large mouth
bass, channel catfish, redear, bluegill, and fathead minnow to stock
our new lake. It was an exciting day in March 2017 when the truck
arrived with some 15,000 fingerlings. Amazingly, our three-inch bass

grew to thirteen inches by November 2017, and our catfish, bluegill, redear, and minnows reproduced several times, with some of the catfish growing from five inches to eighteen inches in length. Some of my most memorable events during the summer of 2017 were helping new fishermen catch their very first fish.

During this time, I struggled with a name for our new lake. After several attempts, my youngest daughter, Marissa, asked me to think about where my grandfather, Stephen, was born. I replied Godstone, England, and she just looked at me until the lights went on, and Lake Godstone came into being.

While Wade and his family built our new lake, dam, and upper-meadow pond, and bulldozed new trails around the lake, the ranch perimeter and interior, Duane was very busy with building the new lodge, the water-storage building, the maintenance shed, the trail showers and restrooms, and the lodge retaining walls.

Along the way, we made a number of changes and improvements to the design work.

Duane, with his years of construction experience, always had great suggestions. His work crew and subcontractors were always very experienced and professional, helping us to plan and to compact the construction process such that the work was substantially complete in about eight months.

I remember standing on the newly constructed second floor of the lodge, looking north through the steel support structure at the hole where the lake would be, and it quickly became obvious that we needed a long window view from there, so Duane suggested a twenty-foot dormer, and the rest is history.

I also wanted a greenhouse on the property, and, like so much that happened during the seven months when I pretty much spent living in the apartment there, I was nudged in the night by my maker and shown what was meant to be. I always knew that what was to be was already in the plan and that I was only there to carry out that plan. God provided me with the vision and left it up to me to figure out how to make it happen. He definitely works in mysterious ways!

Placing the greenhouse on the south side of the lodge and attached to the lodge was yet another afterthought that worked into the process with little interruption. In addition, building an aquaponics garden inside was a natural fit. My son-in-law, Josh, introduced me to his friend, Michael Rosenberger, who had an aquaponics garden at his home in Highland Village, where we lived, and Michael was a tremendous help in designing and building our garden, where fish and vegetables grow together with minimum attention, once balance is achieved.

Wade and family with Jim digging Lake Godstone

I contracted the construction of a 20,000-gallon freshwater drinking tank to be located inside an insulated water-storage building and a solar-energy system, complete with battery storage. We included a connection to Tri-County Electric, but we keep our energy consumption to a minimum with the solar panel system. An essentials power panel provided solar power from the battery to the fridges, the water pump, the microwave, and the coffee machine during power outages. And each living area in the lodge has a solar tube, so that lighting during the day is provided by the sun.

Each window of the lodge has a motorized steel shutter located on the inside to protect against severe weather and burglary. There is a whole-house fan upstairs that can very quickly change out all air inside the lodge.

Most important, the lodge is basically a giant steel storm shelter with highly insulated (foam) walls and ceilings. The zoned multistage air conditioning system can be controlled remotely, as can the video surveillance systems.

The property has a wildlife property tax exemption that significantly reduces the tax burden in exchange for providing an environment to protect and encourage the growth of populations of healthy quail, dove, turkey, and deer, while controlling (by harvest) predator populations of skunk, raccoon, bobcat, and coyotes, as well as feral hogs. We eliminated our hog population by constructing a hog fence around the entire length of our property.

There's something about building that makes you feel more connected to the earth—and to the one who created you. I'm not sure if it's the process of building itself and using your God-given talents and gifts and brain to figure it all out or if it's that we are all simply creators, created in the image of the ultimate creator. We have been created—in order to build.

Ranch Wildlife

One of the wildlife-exemption requirements was that we build and maintain five food plots and three deer corn feeders. This requires annual mowing, plowing, and planting of about six acres of land. Another feature of the property was the massive quantity of very large (tons per rock) limestone. We placed rock at the future shoreline of the lake during its construction and along the spillways. We also used this rock to build a retaining wall twenty-feet tall by one hundred-feet wide, which protected the lodge and the fire pit from the lake. Finally, we used rock to build windbreaks around two campgrounds on top of the dam, which is about 80 feet by 200 feet, with an impressive sunrise view of the wooded valley to the east and the lake to the west.

At the time of this writing, we have hosted retreats of up to thirty-five people for our church, Trietsch United Methodist Church (its staff, choir, men's team, high school youth); my Rotary Club; our friends from the past at Nortex; Biz Owners Ed founders; and numerous family outings. At Thanksgiving of 2017, we held a family retreat, where we christened our new pontoon fishing barge and dedicated Lake Godstone. Going forward, we hope to continue support of our church and nonprofit organizations that we are involved with and to provide that service with a small cost-recovery fee to cover cleaning, laundry, and maintenance. For example, we are working with Keith Martz, the Briarhill Middle School outdoor teacher to train junior high school kids about snakes, tracking wildlife, and fly-fishing.

As I traveled the world, I collected coins and small rocks. When we dedicated Lake Godstone at Thanksgiving in 2017, we tossed the rocks that I had collected into the lake at various locations. When I made the announcement to my family that I would toss both the coins and the rocks into the lake, Sherry (an expert hoarder of family memories) was adamant that I shouldn't do so. My three-year-old granddaughter, Delilah, overheard the conversation and sided strongly with her MiMi.

I replied to Delilah that I would do what I felt I was led to do and that she could scuba dive in the lake when she was older and retrieve them. After a minute of thought, she asked me if she could help me throw them in the lake. We compromised and agreed to keep the coins and to toss the rocks.

Although I sometimes find that I view the construction and development of the Marluc Bella Vita Ranch as a personal accomplishment, I know now that it was intended to be—with or without me.

I like what Teddy Roosevelt said:

"It is not the critic who counts; not the man who points out how the strong man stumbles, or where the doer of deeds could have done them better. The credit belongs to the man who is actually in the arena, whose face is marred by dust and sweat and blood; who strives valiantly; who errs, who comes short again and again, because there is no effort without error and shortcoming; who does actually try to do the deed; who knows the great enthusiasm, the great devotion and spends himself in a worthy cause; who at the best knows in the end the triumph of high achievement, and who at the worst, if he fails, at least fails while daring greatly. Far better is it to dare mighty things, to win glorious triumphs even though checkered by failure, than to rank with those poor spirits who neither enjoy nor suffer much because they live in the gray twilight that knows neither victory nor defeat."

Chapter 53

Trading Securities

Having been blessed with some uninvested cash after we sold Nortex and knowing that my experience level in the world of investing in equities was at best an average rating, I signed up for professional training early in 2014. Over the next twelve months, I attended full-time classes at Online Training Academy in Irving, Texas, and spent my days in trading rooms with some of the best and most knowledgeable instructors in the world, along with more than a dozen other students. It's never too late to try something new or to become better at whatever it is you want to do. You can learn and should strive to learn something new every day.

The classes provided extensive training in the trading of forex, futures, options, and equities, with trading methods for short-term, medium-term, and long-term investing. I graduated with a Master Mind certification, which provided me with a lifetime membership to attend worldwide trading rooms (online) around the clock and to watch and learn or to participate. This training, along with my hands-on, full-time management of our rental real estate portfolio, provides me with the ability to obtain real and true information about world economic conditions. It also has opened my eyes to the dangers of the markets and the regular manipulation of markets by large institutions. The futures market trades twenty-four hours a day, except for weekends, and opens up Sunday afternoon in the United States.

By the time most Americans get out of bed Monday morning, the world markets quite often have already dictated what kind of trading day we'll have in our stock markets. The rise and fall of stocks within a channel trend are the result of institutional traders entering and exiting positions, and they feed on retail-investment fear and greed. As an older investor, I don't have enough time on this Earth to buy and hold, because the next recession might outlast me.

So I spend my trading time (mostly early mornings) in online trading rooms with qualified professionals and day trade and swing trade. However, I tell my children to maximize investments in Roth 401K plans and then IRAs with medium or higher-risk elements and keep buying and holding. Unless you have extensive trading experience, such as what I undertook, you are facing tremendous odds in trying to trade the market successfully.

Chapter 54

Giving Back

"If you wait until you can do everything for everybody, instead of something for somebody, you'll end up not doing nothing for nobody."

—Malcom Bane

My first experience as a young man volunteering for community service was as a Boy Scout leader. Camping back in those days was fun, but you won't catch me sleeping on the ground any longer.

I then became a minor hockey league coach in the Millican-Ogden community in Calgary at age twenty-three. The sports director quickly took me up on my offer to take charge of building our three outdoor hockey rinks. The boards were permanently installed in the fields, so building the ice surface was all that was needed. It was an art to build a good ice surface for hockey and figure skating. I learned from the best, who instructed me to flood the grassy surface long before the air temperature stayed below freezing during the day. Normally, that would be in early December, so the late-night flooding began in early November. It was important that the ground be saturated to a depth below the frost line so that when the weather started warming up in the spring, the underlying frozen soil would keep the ice surface frozen. A good outdoor rink could then be used well into March under normal conditions.

I coached Tiny Mite Hockey, which included boys of nine and ten years old. I liked taking a "C" team under my wing that first year because it was fairly easy to focus on individual development during practice and then work on team skill during the games. The sports director assigned me the traveling "B" team during my second year, and we conquered teams in other communities that our small community had never beaten. I still remember our captain, Timmy

David Hammer, Jim, Jay, and Bettye Rodgers at Biz Owners Ed

Perizollo, scoring in overtime to win a post-season tournament against a much larger community and the very exciting and rewarding feeling it generated in me.

I joined the Lions Club that year and managed a skate-a-thon to help fund our community sports programs. The kids were directed to go door-to-door in our community and obtain commitments for sponsorship on a per-lap-of-the-rink basis. Typically, a boy could skate 500 laps in his assigned time slot and a one-cent-per-lap sponsorship would raise $5.00. Weather was not usually an issue because the show would go on, no matter what the weather was doing. Hockey games were cancelled only if the game time temperature dropped below zero degrees Fahrenheit. We didn't measure in Celsius back then.

We moved to the Fairview Community the next year, which was one of the few communities that had an indoor hockey rink, in addition to outdoor rinks. I became the sports director in my second year there after our elected sports director had a heart attack and died. If my memory is correct, I became sports director when the community association president asked the meeting attendees if anyone was interested in the (volunteer) position and I was the only person with his hand in the air. I found myself at the rink every evening and on the weekends. Fortunately, all three of my children were involved in sports there, so I was with them often.

The next year I was transferred to Spruce Grove, Alberta, by my employer, where I helped coach my daughter, Jennifer, at ringette and my sons, Chris and Tim, at hockey. The hockey season ran from September through April, with lots of opportunities for meeting new parents and community leaders, while sharing a common interest in the activities of our children. I moved my family thirteen times from 1970 through1987, making plenty of new friends along the way, but losing touch with most of them. That's not a good thing.

The economic downturn in the late 1970s forced me to move to Sidney, Montana, to find work. I did my best to start a community hockey program there, and I managed to find city-owned property to put up an outdoor rink. However, when the boards showed up and not a single volunteer agreed to help, I had to give up on the effort. I learned that you must have firm commitments from others before you start anything that requires the help of others. Good deeds rarely go unpunished.

Upon my arrival in Houston, I found that just one minor league boys Tiny Mite hockey team existed in a city of millions of people. The parents were anxious to have a well-trained and experienced coach and gladly paid for our team to fly to Austin, Dallas, and Oklahoma City to participate in regular hockey tournaments. Our team was a mixture of transplanted Canadians and newbie (to hockey)Texans, so the skill levels differed dramatically. We played for the sheer thrill of the game, making new friends everywhere that we traveled.

When I became an American citizen after the ten-year waiting period, I volunteered to run for city council in Highland Village, Texas, in 1992, where we had lived for two years. (www.highlandvillage. org) I won the election and found myself in the middle of numerous issues. We were being unfairly overcharged by the City of Lewisville for utility services, and our shoreline citizens on Lake Lewisville were campaigning hard against a lakeside trail system. We were trying to attract a new junior high school to our city, but the water utility to the land was supplied by the Town of Double Oak, and the water utility had an insufficient supply for a fire-sprinkler system. We were also trying to annex the parkland on the lake adjacent to our city, but the homeowners in the area fiercely opposed our effort. In the end, we were successful in all of these efforts, but it was troublesome to me to experience NIMBY (Not In My Backyard) firsthand.

After my city council term expired, I became involved with a group that was attempting to rescue a performing arts venue in an empty commercial building. I was amazed to see some of our citizens take issue with any effort by the city to start a new teen center in our community. Every effort was made by these people to spread propaganda, including trying to frame the building as environmentally dangerous because it had been used to manufacture ball bearings in its past. In the end, a new nonprofit was formed to buy the building and manage its operation, with a mortgage held by the previous owners.

Some of the land was eventually sold to the City of Highland Village to expand parking for Unity Park, but it took several years to overcome curious opposition. Both Marissa and Luke (our kids) benefitted (along with many other children) from the training in the performing arts center, known as "Studio B," with experts like Scott Foster (television actor) and Annie Wallace (touring with Aladdin). We enjoyed many stage productions over the years, watching our children develop self-confidence, while improving their talent.

Christian Community Action of Lewisville (CCA) was enlarging their housing program for the poor when I served on the board of directors. (www.ccahelps.org) Given my construction experience, I was asked by Tom Duffy, the founder, to manage all elements of the construction process with a full-time, on-site superintendent under my wing. We attempted to utilize volunteer labor as much as possible, but the challenges in doing so were plentiful. It's difficult to fire a volunteer worker who shows up late or endangers others, but we had to do so.

Our existing housing consisted of older homes moved in from close-by lots condemned by the City of Lewisville for expansion of the hospital. It was a good fit, but every home needed extensive remodeling, including new roofs, windows, doors, floor covering, painting, and siding. These construction activities were accomplished with volunteers and donated materials, activities which often would take a very long period of time.

Once the homes were all occupied, we found that one tenant, who had misled us by claiming to be a single parent and unemployed, was actually a gay man with a live-in male friend, and the child was only in his custody for a weekend every two weeks. Our little community was advertised as a temporary refuge for families with children who were financially disadvantaged. As it turned out, both of these tenants apparently had jobs. When we served an eviction notice, they filed a lawsuit under the Federal Housing Act, knowing (apparently) that we had just completed the quantity of housing units necessary to be under federal housing laws. Tom Duffy was furious and immediately closed down one of our unoccupied homes to get us out from under that federal jurisdiction. He had a disdain for anything that involved federal regulation and refused federal funding of any kind because of the "strings" attached to the money supply. Thankfully, Texas had a strong economy, and business owners in our area served on our board, in the food bank, and in the used-clothing store, and they made such generous donations that we didn't need the government in our business. Our efforts were fully focused on serving the poor, instead of filling out forms and being constantly scrutinized by Washington bureaucrats.

We did try to obtain additional funding for our "kids eat free" summer program by applying for a grant to help feed the children of poor families in our community during the summer when parents were working and children were on their own. That funding was approved, but it came with lots of "strings" attached. We could no longer prepare food in our church kitchen, because it was not a licensed food outlet. We could not serve milk, unless we first measured the temperature, ensuring it was within temperature guidelines, and recorded that temperature. If a child only ate a portion of what was served, we could not let another child finish up the meal. The leftovers had to go in the garbage. Worst of all, we were discouraged from religious teachings.

Dorothy Moore was the founder of Reconciliation Outreach, a nonprofit mission located just outside of downtown Dallas. (www.rodallas.org) With housing, a chapel, a kitchen, classrooms, and a gymnasium, the organization served the homeless, the poor, and those who had been recently released from jail. The greatest challenge was driving out the illegal drug presence from the community, and Dorothy excelled in that area. That left the simpler problems, like a bug-bed infestation in the housing units. I was honored to receive the "Divine Servant" award at an annual fund-raiser, but I never did feel quite worthy of that designation because I was surrounded by so many successful people of means who fully supported the organization with their financial gifts.

Children's Advocacy Center is a nonprofit organization that helps to bridge the gap between children who have been sexually abused and the justice-system prosecution of perpetrators of sexual abuse (www.cacdc.org). The focus is on justice and healing, and our community has an outstanding record of prosecution. The operation of the organization is almost fully funded by business owners and people of means. I had the privilege of assisting with the business plan for the addition of a major facility expansion for the organization after a fund-raising effort to ensure that the operation continued to remain debt-free.

Special Abilities is a Lewisville-based nonprofit that provides day care for adults who are unable to care for themselves. (www.specialabilities.net) This service allows their caregivers (usually parents) to work during the day. Funding is largely provided by an annual fund-raiser. As a board member, it is my task to promote the organization and to look for individuals who can contribute to the cost of operations. We were recently able to partner with our church and provide another campus for some of our "Aces."

The Lewisville Noon Rotary meets at Bistecca Steak House in Highland Village, Texas, on Wednesdays. About fifty local friends and business leaders attend regularly, and, after an excellent buffet lunch, a speaker presents us with matters of community interest. The Rotary Club has played a large role in the elimination of polio around the world, and, on a smaller, local scale, our club has adopted an area of FM407 and Garden Ridge to pick up trash on a regular basis. We also undertake many other challenges, such as raising funds for donation to local charity and recognizing special accomplishments of students in the Lewisville ISD. The friendships I have enjoyed at the Rotary Club are an important part of my routine, and I hope to attend until the day I am called away to meet my maker (http://www.lewisvillenoonrotary. org). Giving back is an important part of life, and everyone should do it and experience the joy that giving generates for both the giver and the receiver.

Chapter 55

Persistence

"Nothing in the world can take the place of persistence. Talent will not, because nothing is more common than unsuccessful men with talent. Genius will not, because unrewarded genius is almost a proverb. Education will not, as the world is full of educated derelicts. Persistence and determination alone are omnipotent."

—Calvin Coolidge

"The slogan 'Press On!' has solved and always will solve the problems of the human race."

—Calvin Coolidge

One of the many positive characteristics that define a successful life is persistence, and I would choose persistence over education and life experience every day. Study any accomplishment by another person, and you'll no doubt find that persistence was a key element of goal achievement. Add education and life experience to persistence, and the result will be individuals that will achieve well beyond what is expected of them.

When I experienced bankruptcy soon after a divorce and also unemployment, I chose to face into the headwinds, and, leaning forward into that wind, I placed one foot in front of the other and forced myself to strive forward. The feeling of hopelessness was shoved into the back room of my being with purpose so that my entire awareness was directed at crawling out of a hole. I wasted no time on feeling sorry for myself. Finding a new job, even though it paid a small salary, was celebrated with more-than-appropriate glee. After my car was repossessed, I focused on restoring my old car to running condition and celebrated that achievement as if I had won the lottery. It always amazed me that I could shorten up the time spent on undesirable and unproductive feelings with small, but important, mini-achievements. It's all about attitude and being persistent about your focus and direction.

Now I'm not suggesting that feelings should be ignored. But I do believe that you can redirect emotion with a little practice and a positive mind-set. Sadness and despair can still be expressed and experienced and, no doubt, they should be addressed. However, moving out of reverse and into first gear is far better than moving from reverse gear into park and staying there. I highly recommend moving immediately into overdrive, in a preplanned and desirable direction, one step at a time. Life is about peaks and valleys, and we should strive to overcome adversity quickly rather than get stuck in it (https://youtu.be/hzBCI13rJmA).

Directions

Now that you've gotten this far, I encourage you to think about your own collection of stories. You are the only one who sees the world the way you do and who knows the stories you've lived. How will you capture it for the world? What would you leave behind if challenged to leave a legacy?

I started my book manuscript with three questions.

1. Are you logical and protective, or are you creative and compassionate?
2. What is more important? Is it feelings and emotions, or thoughts and ideas?
3. Which of these attributes should lead our lives, and which should follow them?

Women and liberals (in general) are more creative and compassionate than men and conservatives, while men and conservatives (in general) are more logical and protective then women and liberals. These attributes are in our DNA. Both are necessary for our survival and advancement, of course, and if you don't fit my assessment, don't focus on the definitions. The definitions are generalizations, and I do realize that each one of us is unique.

What I have also noticed is that really compassionate and creative people tend to be somewhat careless and that really logical and protective people tend to be somewhat fearful. Balance is therefore paramount.

Both mind-sets bring much-needed skills to the table. So which one should lead and which one should follow? We need creativity, but we also need logical steps and an action plan to execute any big idea. To answer the question, you first must go through a process of determining what you love doing, what you are good at doing, what you can be paid for doing, and then what the world needs you to do.

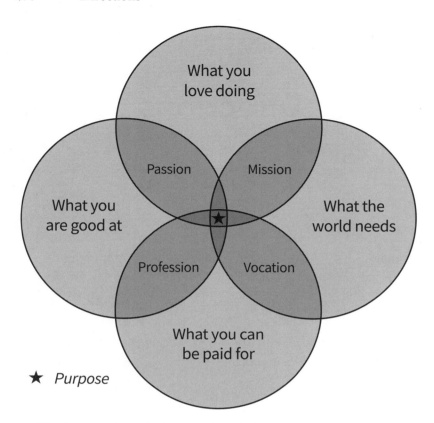

★ *Purpose*

The intersection of what you love doing and what you are good at doing will likely occur first in life, and a passion for that "thing" will develop—whatever it is.

We are all given gifts by God at birth, and determining what those gifts are is often a long (but necessary) discovery process.

The intersection of what you are skilled at doing and what you can be paid for doing is usually dependent on education. For a lot of people, that becomes your profession. Great care should therefore be taken in the selection of your education goal. The greatest failure of education is the pursuit of a profession that lacks that passion.

Hopefully, at some point in your life, you will find yourself at the intersection of what you can be paid for and what the world needs. That is called your vocation. It is critical for our advancement as a species that we all strive for this intersection and recognize the opportunity when it presents itself. And, frankly, your profession and vocation may be the same. I believe that teachers (as an example) nearly always fall into this category. Helping others and lifting them up are essential elements of happiness. However, it is possible that a teacher who doesn't feel an intrinsic connection to the children she or he is teaching simply isn't cut out for that vocation, despite a stellar education. It doesn't matter if you've got an MBA or a PhD in a certain vocation, if you discover you're simply not called to it at all. People can be gifted to pass tests in the medical field, for instance, yet they discover that they abhor working in health care or listening to patients. Since listening is a key component of being a doctor, it would be wise to make a course correction quickly in order to find out what exactly it is that individual was not only passionate about but gifted to do. You can't serve others well in a vocation if you dread going to work every day. You can perform, but just not as well as another person who is passionate about their job.

Discover your passion!

Finally, the intersection of what the world needs and what you love doing will provide you with a mission. Your mission may not occur until late in life as a retirement position. Or it may occur because your skills and gifts have financially compensated your efforts in some way to the extent needed to survive or live the lifestyle that you prefer. If you reach the status in life where you can do what you love doing and that which you do helps others in some meaningful way, well, it just doesn't get better than that, and you shall be richly rewarded when you meet your maker one day.

As I traveled the world from Alaska to Antarctica and China to Russia and just about everywhere in between, I learned a lot about a lot of different things that I would not have otherwise known. There are faces I'll never forget, and lessons entrenched in me I'll share for generations to come. Lessons like kindness have no language barrier, and God meets you everywhere you go.

Anthony Bourdain states it perfectly: "Travel changes you. As you move through this life and this world, you change things slightly, you leave marks behind, however small. And in return, life—and travel—leaves marks on you." Traveling planted me in the middle of other peoples' stories, and their experiences taught me more than I could have imagined. You can get through hard things! I'm the proof!

The world is in constant flux between wars, natural disasters, and personal devastations. You never know what people are facing. Although the changes around the world are real and ongoing, the people are the same underneath the different cultures and languages. What marks will you leave on the world? Better yet, what marks will the world leave on your legacy? Now is the best time to find out.

All this being said, I believe that you should always let logic and protective behavior rule your life while allowing enough room to ignite creativity and compassion for others. The same applies for our leaders. Always follow those that lean toward logic and protective behavior.

This combination and a faith in God is the key to a successful and joy-filled life.

I'd like to leave you with just one short story: Two young men found massive numbers of starfish stranded on a sandy beach after a ferocious storm and the starfish were facing certain death. One of the men started picking up the starfish and tossing them home into the sea. His friend said, "Hey, there are to many of them. What difference will it make anyway?" The man responded by tossing another starfish into the sea and said, "I just made a difference to that one." One at a time. This is your purpose in life. Making a difference in the lives of others. Pure joy at last. May God bless you and guide you and grant you wisdom.